Raising Nobility

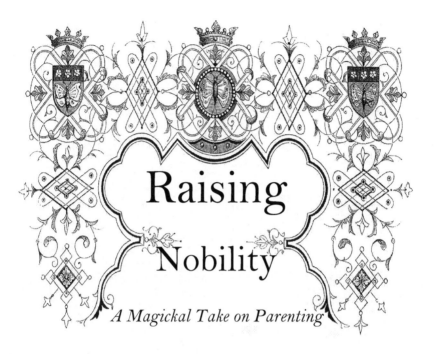

Raising

Nobility

A Magickal Take on Parenting

by

C. JoyBell C.

All books by C. JoyBell C. are printed in the U.S.A.,
Great Britain and Continental Europe.

ISBN: **1500630942**
ISBN- **978-1500630942**

www.cjoybellc.com
authorcjoybellc@gmail.com

*For all
our children.
And for us.*

Introduction

Many of the things that I write were formed from seeds that were born from the thought of what I feel and believe my son needs to know, and secondly, of what I believe all children everywhere should know.

I have spoken of how I envision raising children with nobility, honour and truth. I have a vision of a noble race— that race being all of our children. I imagine children who carry philosophy within their hearts, who ponder upon divine ideas and eternal thoughts; children who know themselves even while they are still learning who they are, because their gaze is always looking inward onto the path of soul-knowledge and mind-mastership. In my mind's eye I see a new race of children who carry a silence within, a place where they are immovable and strong; a new race of children who are developed equally in Will, in Soul and in Flesh, with no part of their trinity being left behind. I picture a powerful new race, a beautiful new race, a race that is gentle but fortified. I see children who are capable of looking beyond what is placed in front of them, who are capable of perceiving the seed in the ground when looking at the centennial tree! I see a race of children with vision that goes beyond and under and over.

I once talked about how wonderful it would be if schools were built to teach the stuff of the soul! Where philosophy would be taught alongside the alphabet and arithmetic, where the Soul is recognized as much as the mind and the flesh are recognized. It is the failure of the human race to develop in a threefold harmony that is the root of all weakness that we witness today. I would say that most people develop in only one area while the other two areas of their existence are left far behind. It is because of this reason that I believe that the old Schools of Mystery were the only true schools. Sometimes, I think that everything we have now is simply a remnant of what once was, that the "schools" we put our children in today are lop-sided institutions that are mere shadows of the great Schools of Mystery that once were the homesteads of Kings and Queens. Meanwhile, as parents we are too busy chasing our own lost dreams to become the temples that our children deserve to attain and to be sheltered in. So you might be wondering, *what would a C. JoyBell C. school be like?* And that is what I hope to reveal to you within the covers of this book.

If I had a school for raising children in, lessons would be taught by highly empathic teachers, those who see and feel beyond the normal range of seeing and feeling. During lectures, the divine thoughts would be pondered upon back-to-back with problems in mathematics and events in history. In my school, truth would not be censored and what is taught would not be predetermined by the government or the church; but what is taught would be the things that bring life to bones and hearth to the Soul! Astronomy would be taught as a way to connect with what is grander than ourselves, thus inculcating humility. The care of animals would be cultivated as a way to see truly beyond our own feelings and thoughts, thus developing empathy and gentle affections. The old arts of magic would be taught in order to exercise the will of the mind, thus forming a strong will that can bend anything in its path! The secret writings from archaic times would be readily available and the children would be taught these old tongues in order to interpret the manuscripts by themselves! But that is what my physical school would be like if I could put one up! However, given the stereotypes, ignorance, fear and stupidity that are all too prevalent in our modern-day societies, I doubt I will ever be able to put up such a physical institution for our age. Not unless there was an extraordinarily drastic change in the world or a total paradigm shift in the universe.

Instead, I know that I must rely on the incorporeal bricks and mortar (oh wow, I just had déjà vu right now while writing this) that I have, in order to build a school that is embodied by the children themselves. And how can I do this? I can only do this by turning the parents into temples, temples that are worthy to be sought, attained; temples that are fortified, firm, equipped to shelter the children inside of them. I must speak to the parents so that they may become the schools for their children.

I believe this is what I have already been doing. You see, when I write things, I don't see only letters and spaces and paragraphs and pages! I don't see only words; but I see buildings and houses, I see castles and fortresses, I see communities and cities! I am a builder and I build things with my words, this is what I do and it is my hope that with this small book I will be able to bring together the materials that are suitable to make the school that I so long to have and that you so wish existed.

I became a mother at a young age. I married at the age of seventeen and had my son later when I was eighteen. I tell him today that I had him so early because I couldn't wait any longer... but this is more than just a cute story. I actually began dreaming about my son years before I met the man whom I would marry! I would see him in my dreams, we were together in my dreams at night! And I had already chosen his name years before I even knew that his father existed on this planet and years before I ever had a boyfriend. He was always with me, even before I met him and I believe that he has been my son throughout many lifetimes prior to this one. I never decided that I would believe in incarnation or reincarnation or the living of multiple lives; I wasn't initiated into a coven or anything like that, but I found that as my life unfurled, I was unwittingly uncovering things that I never used to believe in but that were a part of me!

I believe that the children we bring into the world are more than just our "offspring" we plan to have when we want to have them. I believe that the greatest and most honourable way of creating a better world for the future is by molding better children today. I believe that if you bore a child/children early in life and then spent your younger years raising your son/s and daughter/s while everyone else was busy going to university and climbing the corporate ladder— I believe that work you dedicated yourself to has been worth every minute of it! Raising children with all of your heart is worth it. Molding people and guiding a soul/s who has/have come to you as a source of shelter and care and love— *that* is *so* worth it! I am honoured to be mother to my son and I thank him for that and I thank God for that. We are all honoured to be parent/s to our children and we should tell them that.

My guess is that this book will be unlike any parenting book out there, in that I am reaching down into a very different place than what most are used to even hearing or catching a glimpse of. I reach back to the place of High Mysteries, I reach down into the buried treasure chests of the Mages. Expect something different that will leave you as someone different than who you were before. The book itself is a compilation of some of my teachings that I have gathered for you here into one place. It doesn't necessarily take a thousand-page book to change you; really, all it takes is a few small seeds because sometimes the smallest types of seeds give birth to the mightiest of trees!

The subtitle of this book, *A Magickal Take on Parenting*, incorporates the word "magickal" instead of "magical", in order to differentiate Soul Science from the commonly popular magical parlour games, illusions and stage tricks. Originally, the word was only "magic", but later on there came about the need to differentiate from the olden ways and the newly invented parlour games, stage tricks and illusions. Within these pages though, I am simply using the original term, "magic" to refer to Soul Science/the olden ways, so that this manuscript will be more authentic and less influenced by the modern need to differentiate itself. Please bear this in mind while reading, remember that I am *never* referring to modern games nor to anything you might see on the sidewalk in Vegas or on the T.V. on your favourite entertainment channel.

I am not sure if there is any other book out there that addresses parenting from my perspective, from a perspective of lore, myth and magic. You may consider this work of mine as a grimoire and I so welcome you to step through into a whole new reality! I hope that it will become your new reality, a place that you will never leave!

What must children be made up of, to come into a world like this one? Children must be made up of silk. They must be brought up with serenity in their skin but a bulletproof strength in their souls. This is the new breed of children— ones that are soft to the touch but are truly unbreakable! And unbreakable in a beautiful way; not in a lost way.

Roots and Wings

We are all concerned with raising children "with roots." Someone once said that children are to be raised "with roots and with wings." But what are roots? What is it that we give to children when we want them to grow roots? Well usually we think of "where we came from" and think of inculcating into our children the knowledge of where they came from, which commonly hints at family ties, morality, heritage, surnames and the like. But how deep are these roots, how far do they really go? Do they give our children enough? Is that long enough of a root to reach down and grab all the nutrients from the soil, enough nutrients to take along on the journey of the one who flies with new wings? Another thing that comes to mind when we think of giving our children roots, is our religion. This is very understandable, in that religion, for most people, makes up the very roots of their character, their everyday lives, so on and so forth. And many times, to raise a child in faith is to raise a child in strength and in character. Not always but many times indeed. Why is this? I believe this is because faith has roots that run back into what is ancient. Actually, faith in itself *is* faith. And I believe that faith, in itself, belongs to the spirit of mankind, to the souls of people! That is a faith immovable. But to have a faith in a certain religion is still to have a faith in something, a rock upon which one may build a strong

1

foundation. The failure of this root, however, lies in the fact that religion of today is exoteric rather than esoteric. In other words— the roots are short and the eyes of those peering into it don't see further than what is presented on the surface! Again, we may ask ourselves, "Is this enough?" Do the roots of religion in fact run deep enough? How far deep do they really go? And then you must ask yourself, "How deep should my child/children's roots go?"

I want to see children with roots that run so deep that they could not be dug up by pitchfork nor by crane! Neither by envy nor by hostility! Roots growing so deep that they have wound themselves around holy grails and sacred temples! Hallowed tombstones and divine mysteries! The roots that I want children to have are the roots immovable, the roots esoteric, the ones that reach so deep, you wouldn't be able to find them with your naked eyes! You would need to awaken the eyes of your spirit to find them! The roots of our children must be entwined around the mysteries of old, the questions asked by sages, the answers given by Angels and the philosophies taught by those Great Ones we can only say were half god and half man for their wisdom seeming to sprout from waters most eternal! We must be raising thinkers and seekers, warriors and knights, noble men and queens most beautiful! We must be infusing the blood of our children with blueness, with nobility.

Our children must know themselves. This is the one true religion. Because the Kingdom of God is

Within. Within the human soul, mind, spirit, is the exact reflection of the composition of the Universe around us. The stars and the planets— the worlds— they are the exoteric form of the esoteric that is within us and our children must turn their vision inwards and take that journey into themselves, to know themselves, to be themselves, to stumble upon their true and final purposes in this world! These are the roots that will also give wings! Wings and feathers to fly into the direction of dreams that are dreamt by the immortal spirit! Not dreams that are planted by the television or by magazine columns; but dreams that were dreamt long before your children were even here! Dreams that were dreamt at the very conception of the thoughts of them, the individual thoughts of them that were formed out there in the pools of all that is eternal. These are the roots that bring with them wings.

Saving Our Daughters

I believe that the moment a girl realizes that she is beautiful— she experiences a sacred transformation. I truly believe that beauty holds a sacred place in the throne of woman. We are not born feeling like we are beautiful, or at least, not realizing our full potential/the full potential of our beauty; but there are pivotal points in our lives when our beauty begins to unfurl for our eyes and we realize the extent of its reach therein. These pivotal points are crucial and delicate. I believe that the growth of, and direction taken by, a girl, is greatly determined by these crucial and delicate "zones" created by words, experiences, observations and impressions. And one could argue, *"Something as shallow as beauty?"* but it is nonsense to argue such a thing. The apex of all wisdom and honor is beauty and many an ancient Grecian Philosopher has expressed that. According to those demigods like Plato, beauty is the holy grail of why we search for anything at all! The problem lies in today's modern associations with beauty. People see things so vulgar and ignorantly call them "beautiful." It is the stupidity of man that is shallow; it is *not* beauty that is shallow. Beauty is at the crown, the highest reach of wisdom, honor, gold...

I believe that it is crucial *how* your daughter comes to realize her own beauty. If she comes to associate her own sense of beauty born out of comparisons to other girls; unfortunately, she will continue to glean that by comparing herself to other women throughout her life. We all know this is not a beneficial way to feel that you are beautiful (through comparing yourself to other women)! Now, if a little girl realizes her sense of beauty at an early age, associated with experiences that are innately and eternally strong and fortified (e.g. the realization that the rose is beautiful and that she, like the rose, is a beautiful creation) then her belief in her own beauty will in turn take on that same form— the form of the beautiful creation that she has come to associate herself with/as. Imagine talking to your small child, telling her, "You are as the eternal Sun that rises and sets in the dawns and in the twilights, a beautiful creation unattached from the criticisms and faults of mankind." Just imagine what kind of a woman that little girl will grow up to be! Now think about how useless it is for your daughter to realize her beauty and self-worth based upon what boys think of her or based upon what her friends think of her or what the media thinks of her! If she associates her own beauty with that of what she sees in magazines, on television, or from what kind of "feedback" she gets from boys— she is going to become a woman full of insecurities, not knowing who she really is. If she's not a model— she's not beautiful enough, if she's not sleeping with every guy at school— she's not beautiful enough, if she's not a beauty queen title holder— she's not beautiful enough! These are all false perceptions. Just perceptions. And yet it is these *perceptions* that mold and form our daughters, our little girls!

The key is *not* in training our little girls to care less about being beautiful— that is not the natural order of things! But the key is *being the vanguard* of those very first steps she takes on the journey into seeing and placing her own beauty, her own attractiveness! She doesn't need to be only beautiful on the inside and not on the outside; but like the sunshine, she can be worthwhile, useful and meaningful, while bringing beauty to the dawns and to the dusks! What do our little girls equate beauty with? With creations in the sky everlasting, like the stars and the Moon? With the beautiful constellations? Or do they only know what is beauty to the swine? The title of "beautiful" in exchange for sex, in exchange for attention, in exchange for making money for huge companies? Think about it. Really think about it.

When you look at your beautiful daughter or niece or little sister— associate her with things immortal— *and tell her that.* Bring her belief in her beauty up so high that it exceeds the reaches of mankind's mortality and lies. *Save your little girls.*

And what about *you?* You the mama? You the grown woman? Do you look back at the first conceptions of beauty in your mind, at those first perceptions of yourself that you had and think to yourself, *"It's too late for me"?* But no, it is never too late for one who is able to reach down into herself, know herself, know her soul and *remake the fabric of her own spirit from the inside-out! You can change yourself, in your own eyes, by your own efforts!* Take yourself back to when you were a little girl, speak to yourself, comfort yourself, *see yourself!* See yourself beautiful!

All the evil in the world rejoices when a beautiful woman looks in the mirror and does not see her worth. Overcome that evil a little more every day, by seeing and acknowledging your worth, your value, your beauty and not only doing this for yourself but also doing this for the ones you love.

"And the true order of going, or being led by another, to the things of love, is to begin from the beauties of earth and mount upwards for the sake of that other beauty, using these steps only, and from one going on to two, and from two to all fair forms to fair practices, and from fair practices to fair notions, until from fair notions he arrives at the notion of absolute beauty, and at last knows what the essence of beauty is."
(Plato, *The Symposium*)

"Beholding beauty with the eye of the mind, he will be enabled to bring forth, not images of beauty, but realities (for he has hold not of an image but of a reality), and bringing forth and nourishing true virtue to become the friend of God and be immortal, if mortal man may."
(Plato, *The Symposium*)

"...when he looks at Beauty in the only way that Beauty can be seen - only then will it become possible for him to give birth not to images of virtue (because he's in touch with no images), but to true virtue (because he is in touch with true Beauty). The love of the gods belongs to anyone who has given to true virtue and nourished it, and if any human being could become immortal, it would be he."
(Plato, *The Symposium*)

Saving Our Sons

I have met men who are only capable of feeling a sense of self-worth when they are able to count the number of women who are attracted to them and from thereon, gauging by the age and appearance of those women, including just how much those particular women are attracted to them, they glean their own sense of worth and respectability. The problem here is that usually men who are under the influence of such a mindset are individuals who are not actually doing anything with their lives to make themselves worthy of anyone or anything greater. They base their value upon what kind and how many women they can sack; meanwhile, they are doing nothing with their lives or with their characters in order to actually be considered respectable members of society. But this is also due in part to the fact that there are many women who throw themselves onto men who don't even deserve them. When you give a crown to a chimp, I'm sure the chimp will believe he deserves that crown! This doesn't actually mean that he does! And where does this female behavior/lack of better judgment come from? Well it still stems from the fact that there are too many women who don't know their worth, in the first place. They think that they need to sack every guy that comes their way/ they are just plain lascivious, hence ending up giving fake crowns to false princes! What happens when the women are taken away and the fake crowns fall to the ground? What kind of a man is left standing under all of that? Because that's who a man truly is.

Our boys must be raised cultivating their own talents, dreams and aspirations... our boys must be raised as builders, as creators! We must raise our boys into men who have built for themselves a very strong and very immovable foundation within them, we must raise whole men; not just men who are a half of a man and need to fill the other half with temporary people and temporary things! Why are we doing the boys of our world such a disfavor? Why?

Too many men these days function as mere *things* and not as individual people! Because it is the person who gives value to the thing; it is not the thing that gives value to the person! And yet our men grow up looking outward for women to grab onto, to fill their inner selves with! As if they themselves are not people but as if they need other people to validate the value of their own worth. They seek outwardly what they deem can give value to them inwardly! They rely on empty promises from other empty souls, only to find themselves baking in a pie of lies. The world is raising pie-men! Nothing but pies! When we should be raising fine fortresses with pillars of marble and walls of stone! We must raise our boys into men of substance and value, into men who have substance and value *on their own*; not because they have reached out and added that to them, from external sources. We find so many, many broken men because there are too many, many men who have lost a greater part of themselves because they put that greater part of themselves into external people and things. Those things and those people, once gone, take those parts with them, never to be returned!

We need to raise lighthouses— men who can stand as beacons of light on rocky cliffs in the middle of hurricanes and thunderstorms! But look all around us now! What kind of men has the world raised? I have met so very, very few men in my life whom I can truly say are admirable, whom I can say I admire and would aspire to become like, as a person. Instead, the world has raised men who are afraid and abandoned and confused. Men who would want to be kings simply by renting a throne and donning a bed sheet as a robe! Men who would want to be kings simply by raising their feet up and placing themselves on a pedestal of their imagination! A cardboard box that they imagine being a pedestal of jade and jasper! Men who want to pretend their ways into existence!

I have raised my son into a young man of substance, gratitude, strength, vision and honour. So God wills it to be. But I also want you to be able to raise your son in the ways that I have raised my own young man. I want you to raise sons unbreakable, fortified and true. I want us all to raise outstanding citizens, exemplar role models, lovers, friends and fathers. We build the pillars of the world as we build our young men. Show your sons their worth, tell them of all the things that they can do, tell them stories of their own strengths, of their own victories! Build your young boys upon foundations of their own achievements, victories and strengths. Raise young boys upon the principles of fortitude and gentleness, upon the principles of patience and self-sacrifice.

And what about you? You the father, the uncle, the grandfather? The big brother? Do you think that your time is up? Nay, go back to unearth the useless stones that were once laid and replace them with slabs of jasper and jade.

Who Is Your Hero?

When I was a little girl, just like any other little girl, I looked around for a role model I felt like I could look up to, I looked around for someone that could make me feel like I knew who I should be and in fact be it! But when I couldn't find that person; I instead decided to *become* that person.

Young children grow up wanting to be able to look up to somebody, wanting to have somebody there whom they can aspire to become just like. You see it in the mainstream media all the time— girls and boys trying to emulate people in pop culture and their outraged parents attacking those figures for "not being good enough role models." I too, went through a stage when I would pick out somebody to emulate and those somebodies would come from t.v. shows, characters in books, characters in movies... people who all had absolutely nothing to do with me, didn't know I existed and were just working to earn their own livelihood. In other words, nobody that I should have had any business emulating!

When we are young children, we want the people of the world to be bright and shining stars that we can imitate and become just like! And you know, I am happy for the children of the world who have been fortunate enough to have true role models to emulate, especially the ones who were born into outstanding families, to fabulous parents, who are surrounded by incredibly genuine and beautiful relatives and friends. There are such people that are alive in the world and I am very happy for them. But such is not the case for many people and such was not the case for me. Now, I am not saying that I was not born into an impressive lot, because I was, but I am just saying that I could not find amongst my family, a woman whom I felt I wanted to emulate and become just like. There was my grandmother, Leona (she had a beautiful name that means "lioness"), who I can say would definitely fit that role, but seeing as she was my grandmother and represented a later era in the life of a woman, I still couldn't relate myself to wanting to become just like her in terms of being a young woman. My mother, Deogracia (doesn't she have a beautiful name, it is Latin for, "God's grace") is an exemplar woman, herself. She is a pianist, fine artist, a hard working businesswoman who dedicates her life to philanthropy and to her faith. But still, her and I are called forth onto paths so dissimilar that I still could not see her as someone I wanted to be just like. In fact, I never really could feel like I "fit in" to my family from either side (both maternal and paternal). A big factor in my feeling this way is the fact that I am the only predominantly multiracial person in my family, so far. They just all look the same and I just look so different from them!

Though I cannot say that I was given the best lot in life when it comes to noble and loving bloodlines, I can say that I do understand why that was not given to me. I can see and perceive that if my life with my family had been any better than it was while I was growing up, I would probably never abandon many of those attachments in favour of seeking and searching. "Seeking and searching for what?" you may ask, and what I mean is seeking and searching for that thing which was missing. It is because of that lack and want that I have sought out the missing pieces of me. If I had ever felt like I utterly belonged and was accepted, then I would not forage for divine secrets hidden in obscure places. Why would I do that if everything in my life had been perfect? I wouldn't! Because I would be content, I would feel like I already belonged! But it is because of my scouring for whom and for where I really belong, that I have found the tools to make myself out of. I have found Elementals and Angels, Gods and Elves! I have found faith unlike any presented to me as a child! I have found my true family to whom I belong.

So like I said, later on as a teenager I would try to mold my ideal person out of the characters I would discover through literature and media. For example, my then favourite novel, *Little Women* by Louisa May Alcott, features four young women, from whom I chose two to represent who I was/ what I was like! I chose Jo and Amy and I even called the new creature "JoAmy" in order to embody the person that I was (Jo was a tomboyish writer while Amy was a feminine and materialistic dreamer).

As I grew into a young woman, more and more, day by day, I became increasingly aware of the fact that I was no longer able to find a person that I could emulate.

Nobody could be my hero, nobody was there to "take me by the hand" and guide me towards things like self-worth and personal development. I wanted to be so much more and I just couldn't find someone who could play the role of an adequate role model for me. That's when I decided to become what I couldn't find. That is when I became the person who I wanted to find!

I believe that our children today are capable of becoming and of being the person that they want to look up to! Yes, it is difficult. Sometimes it is even very difficult. But it is a victory when achieved and it is not only a victory when achieved, but it is a magnanimous testament to the strength of the will, the strength of the individual's perception, focus, stamina and stability of mind and of soul! Our children are capable of keeping a vision in their minds of whom they want to become, what they want to be like, and then they are capable of keeping that in focus even when it is not present in front of their physical eyes! They are capable of creating this vision in their mind's eye, contouring and developing this vision with their willpower, until they become what it is that they have kept in focus. Now what exactly am I talking about here? Well ,I am talking about specific things like the character of the individual, the personality. I am talking about how the person talks, dresses, walks and thinks! And laughs!

We are all capable of becoming our higher selves— the selves that are free from tears and fears lingering within and around the aura, the selves that do not falter and second-guess themselves every single step of the way! We can all become the kind of people who are kindhearted, self-assured, accomplished and hardworking. The kind of people who make a difference and who aren't going to be forgotten so easily, not ever! But first we have to all be brave enough to lean on ourselves instead of onto the images we bear in our minds of the outlines of other people! Yes, the very first step is to do a "trust test" and fall backwards into *your own* arms, trusting that *you* will catch *you!* You become you, for you! And because you love other people. Because the best way that we can love the people who love us is by waxing into our own higher persons. Moreover, when we embark on the journey of becoming our own heroes, we are shedding our own insecurities and feelings of inadequacy, in the process. And when you think about it, it is actually rather cowardly to make a role model out of somebody else instead of yourself! You get to put all your expectations onto someone who doesn't even know you, you get to calculate outcomes and imagine successes based upon a person who doesn't even know you are alive! When they make mistakes, the whole world blames them and nobody's going to blame you, of course! In fact, maybe even when you make your own mistakes, you're going to blame them instead of blaming yourself! What an empty way of living. And what a brave way to live when you finally decide to become the person that you want to be! At the end of the day, you are the person who can turn yourself into the person that you want to be.

I grew up listening to my parents complain about how their parents weren't the role models nor the people that they should have been. I grew up listening to both of my parents complain about how they could have been so much better people if only their parents this...if only their parents that. "If only my mother hugged me and told me that she loved me, I would be such a secure person right now", "If only my father were not so harsh on me, I wouldn't need to fight these feelings of inadequacy every day right now". If only, if only, if only... so many "if onlies"! I grew up listening to that, all the time! And while my parents chose to dwell on the past, they neglected their need and opportunity to become for me the parents that they never had! What a waste of opportunity! What a waste of negative energy that could have been transmuted into a positive outcome! I could say the same about them, right now! I could choose to spend my days sitting around and saying the same things they said about their parents! I could choose to say, "If only my parents weren't so busy dwelling on the past and complaining about their own parents, they could have taken the opportunity to be to me the parents that they never had and I would be such a secure and confident individual right now!" I could choose to do that instead of being for my own son, the parent that I once needed! I could choose to do that instead of becoming and being the hero that I looked for and wanted to have! I could choose to do that, rather than being C. JoyBell C. and writing this book that you hold in your hands right now! I could choose to do that. The only difference is that I don't.

"In changing the base metals into gold and silver by the projection of the Stone, it follows (by an accelerated process) the method of nature, and therefore is natural."
— Petrus Bonus Lombardus; *The New Pearl of Great Price*, 1338 AD

Nothing To Fear

I talked to my nephew today, he's afraid of the dark. Or was. I said, "Why are you afraid of the dark? In the darkness we find many beautiful things!" He said, "Like what?" And I said, "Like the Moon and the stars! We would never see them without the darkness! And have you ever been to a movie house before? Do you think it would be as fun if it weren't dark inside? And all the creatures under the sea— they're always there, swimming beautifully in the darkness of the waters!" Then I turned to my son, who is thirteen, and asked him, "What other great things can be found in the dark that we can't have in the light?" "Shadow puppets!" my son replied, and we began making shadow puppets on the cabinet doors, I made an alligator and my nephew made a bunny and he said, "Bad things like ghosts are just fairy tales, right?" Then I told him, "Even if there were ghosts all around, they would not change in the darkness; they would be just the same as they are in the light. Look, we live in a world where there are bad things but there's no difference between these things whether they are in the darkness or in the light! Everything good and bad is always there; what changes is what and when we can see them. And the darkness brings us many beautiful experiences that we wouldn't be able to see in the light." And then I gave him a piece of my son's meteorite, I told him that whenever he feels afraid in the dark, he can hold onto it and it should remind him that many beautiful things, like that meteorite, come from the darkness so there's really nothing to ever be afraid of!

We all talk so much of how and where to "draw boundaries" when it comes to protecting our children. We don't want to "overshield" them from the world; and yet we know that we *are* their shields to many extents! We can be obsessed with shielding them from darkness, yet paradoxically, we sit beside them, watching them fall prey to fear as if fear is "just a part of growing up." But fear should not be seen as "just a part of growing up;" fear needs to be seen as the vanquisher of kings and queens, as the reason why people fall weak, as the root of hindrances in life! We cannot silently sit by as our children tremble in fear of the dark! And yet it is not the darkness that we need to be shielding them from. Children must know that even in darkness, there is nothing to fear!

One thing that I have always guarded my son from— is fear. I myself battled with fear as an adult and through that battle I came to know its form and feel, even the very way that it smells! When you know something because you have battled with it— this is when you can overcome it. Only the courageous can face their own demons and look them in the eyes, subdue them by knowing them and command them by name. I believe that many battles that I have fought have been fought for my son. There is no harm and no shame in fighting battles for your children and one thing I believe we must strive to protect our children from— is fear. Do not take it lightly and do not laugh at it. Put an end to it.

What is Beauty?

What is beauty? In this day when everything and everyone is clamoring for attention, recognition, remembrance and reverence... beauty is what makes the noise go away. Beauty is what makes the noise fade into the background, calls you by your native name and in your mother tongue, woos the threads of your soul and then weaves them together. Beauty is what makes the lies go away and makes everything that is not truly beautiful— fade away. Beauty is sublimity, it is constant and it is an eternal breath. Immovable. Forever. It is the unceasing pattern which designs itself into an invincible quilt that is the true fabric; while all else is simply an accent, a vandalism, a passing thing. Beauty is remembered when it is *not* seen, just as much as it is thought of when it *is* seen. Beauty is almost nothing of all the things that you see on a daily basis! Many of the things you call "beautiful" are a blasphemy. And yet, she (beauty) lingers in places where you would not normally think to look for her! Alas, beauty is only for the eyes that are worthy of her! Her presence alone calls upon reverence, her breath on the air is the cause of things most sublime. And yet she barely knows of her own stature; lowly, she enters into the quietest of recesses, the indwelling where most would tend not to look! She will not be found amongst the noise made by those who seek attention; for those sounds are a wreckage to her serenity. She cannot be found amongst those who shout from the rooftops, for those calls are hellish to her senses. But she will walk by one day and you will remember her forever after that. Once she has touched your life, her fingerprints are unfading!

Our daughters must be raised to see beauty, to know beauty, to *be* beautiful. We must whisper things into their ears— words of reassurance— words that raise their awareness to the true standard of what Beauty is. We must raise our daughters in a way that they will have spirits so immovable that they are unable to be provoked by external stimuli, unable to be provoked by peer pressure, by the voice that tells them they are not beautiful enough unless they compete with that woman, unless they sleep with that man, unless they are seen in that club, on that platform, on that pedestal! We must raise women onto the pedestal of True Beauty, which stands high out-of-reach of the hands of all the lies that would try to pull it down! We must raise daughters with souls so strong that they can be rivaled only by the majesty of the untouchable mountains! Spirits so fortified that are rivaled only by the farthest reaches of the Sun!

And if you think that True Beauty is only for our daughters and not for our sons, think again! But our sons must be raised to have a beautiful countenance, too! To be like ivory tusks prominent against a backdrop of wood! Our sons should be sensitive to the cultivating of the beauty of their own will and countenance, for upon this True Beauty will stand the forms like golden idols,

the golden idols that they build as testament to their
visions, their beliefs, their attainments, their affections
and their continuing journey towards perfection of spirit,
body and soul. For a man must be beautiful, too! A man
must be able to look into the mirror, into his own eyes
and see the fulfillment of his visions as well as the battles
he has won! We often forget that upon the pillar called
man, the world has been built, and society often forgets
the importance of raising our boys into something most
beautiful! Nay, but the soul of a boy must be honed and
sheltered, grown and loved! A boy must be loved into a
knight; he must be grown into a king and led into the
fortresses of his own soul! So may we look upon our sons
and see them in all the original beauty that they have
come to us as, may we look into our sons and see all the
beauty that they have and will have and let us be their
temples until they have built themselves into temples of
their own, let us be their shelters forever, always a place
to return to and come home. May we love our sons into
full beings, may we pave their ways for them, and may
we help them, love them.

A Breath and a Vision

Beyond objectification and sexualization lie the sublime beauty, form and purpose of the female body. I admire the man who is cultured enough to appreciate this; I appreciate the man who, upon looking at the female form, sees it not merely for the exoteric but also for the esoteric nature of what it is; the man who gazes upon the female and sees her for her sublimity and purpose, in her state of goddesshood. I appreciate the man who looks upon a woman and sees a companion, a better half.

In this world that we live in, the "appreciation of the female form" is maligned in the minds of too many men to mean something that it is not. To "appreciate woman" means pornography, objectification, means "the more women the better"! The godhood in man has been lost and along with it, the reign of woman is also now long gone! Empty shells see nothing else but empty shells and appreciate nothing else but the reflection of emptiness projected from their own nature.

In this world that we live in, the woman sees herself as something which must be satisfactory to man; not something which must be satisfactory to herself and to her own standards. The woman today has no standards; her standards are whatever he wants! The once goddess has become now merely mortal, slave to her mortal counterpart.

I see a world wherein goodhood reflects upon godhood and sublimity radiates upon sublimity. I see a world where man is not rat, is not donkey, is not pig. I see a world where woman is not subdued, is not sex toy, is not mere object. This world that I see is one we do not live in, is air we do not breathe, is vision we do not have. How can we breathe to life, from a breath that is not there; create reality from vision that does not exist? Alas, you now have the breath and you now have the vision! Go forth! Go forth and produce heirs to thrones! Go forth and wield Kings out of boys! Go forth and craft Queens out of babies! Raise your boys to be lovers of woman in her true form, raise your girls to be lovers of their own true form. May your bloodline be blessed and may your blessings be multiplied!

A Warning Against Lesser Magic

The manipulative person is the ultimate coward. When you want something, it takes things like perseverance, will power, bravery, sincerity, truth and honour to make that thing happen, to make that thing materialize into a reality. Manipulation is the tool of the coward because, through it, he constructs ways to get what he wants without the use of any of the things that he is not brave enough to produce from within himself. And why do those materials like perseverance, will power and etc. require courage to bring forth? Well ,they are not easy to come by, in the first place. Moreover, you have to truly face the possibility of failure when striving to achieve these things in order to reach what you want. Facing the possibility of failure is the ultimate act of courage. The manipulator cannot face that possibility and that is why he takes all of his ulterior routes to get the things that he wants, routes that do not require anything magnanimous of him. He knows not courage, he knows not inner strength, he has no honour and he cannot even see his own reflection when he looks into the mirror. He sees a reflection of all the things he has patched together, like a collage of cut-outs from magazines stuck onto a corkboard on the wall— it is not himself, but it is what he wants to think of himself as. This is yet another form of cowardice! The inability to look at oneself in the mirror and see who he or she truly is. Why this fear? You must know that to look at one's true reflection would be to see all the things that one doesn't want to see— to see the *truth untainted.* Only the courageous can face their own demons and look them in the eyes, subdue them by knowing them and command them by name!

The manipulator never really gets anything he really wants. And why? Because everything that he does get is not what he really wants. He does not know what he really wants, because he does not even know himself. And so there are things raked in through manipulations— all of these things fall down into a dark hole, a pit that cannot ever be filled. Not until the curtains of cowardice are pulled back.

Why do we raise cowards? Why have we taught our children the ways of the rats and the swine? Why are we afraid to teach our sons and daughters to look at themselves in the mirror and to see their true selves? Why do you not tell your children the stories of old magic, these stories of Divine inquisitions of one's own soul? But all our children are initiates into life and we are the ones who ought to be initiating them, providing them with paths, with means, with ways, and I do not mean paths and means and ways of the cowardly; but I mean paths of strength, means of the noble mind, ways of the true Elven heart! Why do we teach them that magic is not real? Nay, but magic is the true way where nothing can pass into but the truly brave, the courageous ones!

Instructions

There needs to be a silence within your mind, your spirit, your soul. There must be an epicenter filled with silence wherein you can hear clearly the directions given to you, hear the instructions of your teachers so you can see clearly which paths are yours to take. This silence must be kept in focus at all times; this place must never be filled with noise. What is noise? Noise is the relentless seeking of pleasure, the promise of pleasure that the world offers, the laughter, the distractions, the unreal things that are presented to your eyes and other senses, the *panem et circenses*. Noise is the overstimulation of the senses which is a poisoning, an intoxication. This is all light. In the light there is noise and that is why too often the lights in your life are turned off in order to recreate that initial silence and in these instances, unfortunately, pain and hurt become your teachers. Loss and lack become your guides. Because when the lights are turned off, you begin to reach out and grasp, you finally begin to try to see, try to listen! Darkness recreates that silence. But it doesn't need to be that way! You can keep your quiet in focus, always. You can keep that place where the noise is not let in, where the illusions and the distractions cannot find their way into. The emotional provocations can't find their way in there. That room of indifference, of silence and of power. The world has always told you and probably will always tell you, that your power is found in your passion and that your fuel is found in your fire; but this is not truth. Let he who is not meant for truth believe their fabrications and let he who is destined for truth, find it and have it. Fuel is *not* found in the fire. Fuel is found in your ability to contour the fire. Your passions will lead to your imprudence and to your destruction, if you do not possess the ability to contour it, to ride upon the back of the fire-breathing dragon with ease and with aplomb! If you keep that room of indifference inside of you always— even when the lights are on— then no one needs to come in and turn the lights off for you. You can choose your teachers, we choose our teachers! We can *choose* whether pain teaches us or joy teaches us, whether hardship teaches us or gentleness teaches us. Darkness comes to wake us up to the silence; but we can stay awake even in the light, we can choose not to be intoxicated, we can choose not to be poisoned, we can listen always, in the quiet within, to the voices of our teachers, directing us onto which paths to take, showing us the signs. You keep on inviting darkness into your life by being a slave to pleasure and stimulation, by being a slave to your reactions to stimuli. Stop it now! It is time to wake up to silence.

In the midst of your laughter, in the midst of your joy and light— there must be a hollow place, a place of absolute indifference, a place where you are immovable. In the midst of laughter and mirth— hear the quiet voices of your teachers— the ones that lead you, guide you, show you the signs, the directions, the paths which are yours to take.

Pleasure must be something that is beneath your will-power, that is beneath your ultimate call, that is beneath your silence, something which does not direct nor control your senses! The man who is weak in his senses, is held back by these and is prisoner to these! The person who is provoked by outward stimuli is prisoner of this world and of other people while the Master is the one who commands his feelings and his senses. Do not be prisoner to your flesh; but may your flesh follow your will and be guided by your soul.

Our society has taught us to break the will of our children and yet in that very same light it has seduced them into becoming consumers of whatever they want for them to consume! Our very own society has in fact become the noise which drowns out the silence within our children, whilst simultaneously breaking their strong will by teaching us parents and instructors and teachers that we ought to break a child's will, bend it, in order to make it conform to rules and to regulations! But the true rule and the true regulation is not what they have set! The true rule and regulation is the rule and regulation of silence. Silence is a great law. There are many laws, which are not actual laws; but silence is a true law! Take this silence away and you will introduce the teachers called sorrow and pain! Leave the children to their inner silence cultivated by their own strength of will and watch them grow into all that they were meant to be! Teach them where the noise is coming from, expose the nature of that noise and let them fight it on their own, with the strength of their own silence. The strong will of a child must not be broken; but must be shown what is worth fighting for!

Panem et Circenses is a Latin phrase meaning "Bread and Circuses", which is a metonymic for a superficial means of appeasement. A distraction, a diversion, a shallow means of satisfaction and contentment.

You Are Silk

When my son was around eight or nine-years-old, we had an issue with someone in his classroom who had a domineering, manipulative personality. I sat down to talk with him about it and that conversation led to what has become a letter which has been passed from one hand to another, all around the world, touching the hearts and changing the minds of many different people. I want to share that conversation with you here; this is what I said to him:

"You're going to meet many people with domineering personalities: the loud, the obnoxious, those that noisily stake their claims in your territory and everywhere else they set foot on. This is the blueprint of a predator. Predators prey on gentleness, peace, calmness, sweetness and any positivity that they sniff out as weakness. Anything that is happy and at peace they mistake for weakness. It's not your job to change these people, but it's your job to show them that your peace and gentleness do not equate to weakness.

I have always appeared to be fragile and delicate but the thing is, I am not fragile and I am not delicate. I am very gentle but I can show you that the gentle also possess a poison. I compare myself to silk. People mistake silk to be weak but a silk handkerchief can protect the wearer from a gunshot. There are many people who will want to befriend you if you fit the description of what they think is weak; predators want to have friends that they can dominate over because that makes them feel strong and important. The truth is that predators have no strength and no courage. It is you who are strong, and it is you who has the courage.

I have lost many a friend over the fact that when they attempt to rip me, they can't. They accuse me of being deceptive; I am not deceptive, I am just made of silk. It is they who are stupid and wrongly take gentleness and fairness for weakness. There are many more predators in this world, so I want you to be made of silk. You *are* silk."

It is important that we raise children spun from chords of silk, soft and unbreakable. It is equally important that we weave ourselves out of that same fabric, or rather, weave ourselves into it.

Raising a New Race

They have taught us that in order not to be manipulated— we must learn the ways of manipulation! They have taught us that in order not to be victimized— we must prey on a cobra and wear its skin on our heads! They have taught us that if we do not want to get lost in this world, we must draw its alleyways and darkest corners on the backs of our hands! And so they have raised a generation of individuals who take pride in knowing how to camouflage, they have raised a generation of people who take pride in the number of potions they carry in their pockets, in how well they can hide cards up their sleeves! They have raised up an era of people who take pride in the lesser magic— tricks and illusions of the mind! Like blind asses the masses are led astray!

They have mastered the illusions of others and yet they have not looked into the mirror to master themselves! They know the "darkness" of the world? It is written upon the backs of their hands? And yet they do not know the darkness of their own hearts! The truth is that the only darkness that must be mastered is the darkness of one's own heart! For who can dispel the vile creatures if he cannot call them by name? Who can command the ferocious lion, but the one who has given him a name? And yet their lions go unnamed and their monsters roam around in the dark rooms and hallways of their minds and hearts! Rooms and hallways that they do not walk into, they do not look into! And all the while, they are seduced by noise— they laugh and they make merry, they party and they dance! They think themselves seducers of all, and yet all of them see themselves as seducers of all men and women— they are all the same! And only the one more ruthless has any power over all the rest, for it is in this only, this illusion, that they have any power at all!

Why are we not raising a new generation of knights? A new generation of noble ones who know how to wield their flaming swords? Let us raise a new generation that is victorious not by adaptation; but by rising above! Victory by the overcoming of this world! Not by the subjugation to it! As the people take pride in their camouflages, our children will see them as nothing but people running around in the jungle wearing animal furs! It is time for this Neanderthal generation to fade into extinction and it is time for an Angelic Race to emerge! A race of children from all colors and all walks of life who see beyond what is shown to them, who feel the thoughts of others, who perceive intentions, who foresee motives! And our children will overcome them not by becoming like them; but our children will overcome them through *sight!* We will raise seers and overcomers! We will raise intuitive conquerors unafraid of their own demons, for these demons they have bound and subdued!

Queen

My mother used to tell me, "Don't give 100% of your heart to any man, you always have to love yourself more." Fast forward decades into my future and you'll find a me that doubted those words. Eventually you buy in to the desire to fall in love completely with a man and we can all see the "advice columns" of "dating experts" trying to teach women everywhere, how to "make men" do this and "make men" do that— basically, the focus is on how to make a man want you as much as you want him. This idea alone is a misdeed towards all women, everywhere. To make it look like women should be trying to make men want them, is an illusion, is fake, is propaganda. The truth is that you are eventually going to learn my mama's words for yourself and her words are true because men don't really fall in love with you because of your actions; men fall in love with you because of their own actions that *they've* given to *you*. They base your quality upon their own willingness to give, their own willingness to make space for you, to let you in.

You just can't do anything drastic for a man; he's not going to value that. A man is going to value the drastic things that *he* does for *you!* There are plenty, plenty, millions of women who are willing to do drastic things for a man and it is those same women who are easily forgotten, easily left on the sidelines... they didn't even know their own worth to begin with! They dig the same hole for themselves over and over and over again! The idea is not to be one of those plenty, plenty, millions of women! The idea is to be unforgettable.

"How do I be unforgettable? How do I make a man think this and that about me so he'll know I'm worth doing drastic things for?" But those are erroneous questions. *You* need to know that *you* are unforgettable, that *you* are worth it, that *you* shouldn't be bent! Who cares what a guy thinks? Most men gauge what is in front of them based upon what they've been through in the past— much of the time, they're not even equipped to see you because they're looking at you through eyes stuck in the past! *You* have to be present in *your* here and now— for *yourself!*

Too often, us women, we are seduced by the idea of love, of falling in love, being in love, feeling like we are in love and we want to feel the butterflies and we want to feel special and adored... we want these things so much that we go chasing after demons made out of shadows! Most of the time, guys are just people who are messed up and sometimes even more messed up than we could *ever* be! It's a surprise to find that out, isn't it?

My mother was right. I mean, my mother hasn't been right about every single thing; but she has been right about this thing. Don't give your 100% to a man— ever— because it leaves no space for *him* to put in *his* percentage! And if he doesn't see *himself* in there, in any percentage of that, then he just won't see himself there at all. It is a harsh reality to find out that we really aren't

Disney Princesses; but it's more like each of us are our own individual Queens! We go through life needing to remember that we have crowns and thrones and that no matter what happens— those crowns are there, those thrones are there— calling us to live lives full of grace, honour, truth and strength.

Your daughters need to know that they were born with missions and with honour, no matter the circumstances of their conception and birth. Girls have missions to fulfill and yes, it would be a great blessing to have a partner to fulfill those missions with; but that isn't always needful. We create need in our minds and we pass those needs on to our offspring and to the other people close to us in our lives. But it isn't needful to have a partner to fulfill our missions with. You may think that your task in life is to fall in love, to be in love, to be with the one whom you came here for! And that may still be part of your story, or it may even be the case entirely (in some cases, I guess), but consider the possibility that the mission you have to fulfill is something that was given to you because you are equipped to fulfill it, because it was written and what is written will surely be done. Let us please raise our daughters to be seekers of the secrets of their own souls.

Rose Quartz

It has taken me a very long time to see that romance is not really something that should "happen" to you; but that it is an aura, which you should enwrap yourself with, bringing it into your life from the inside-out!

When we think of romance, our first thoughts are of another person bringing that into our lives and that is the natural way of thinking. Or should I say unnatural way of thinking because it is the result of how we were trained to think? We were trained by movies, t.v. shows, literature and pictures streaming through our Facebook timelines, to see and understand romance as something that means someone comes into your life and suddenly you feel like you are so worth it and you are happy and beautiful because someone brings you roses and holds your hand while you stroll along under the moon. That's how we see romance.

But then it hit me! And I stood there and I let it hit me! The veils covering my eyes from the truth were torn down and I saw and I understood that romance is actually a spirit that you have to cultivate within yourself! You need to create romance as a way of living your life. You need to wear pink rose perfume and you need to put on beautiful clothes *because they make you happy* and you need to be in love with the moonlight and the sunshine because of how it feels on your own skin every day and every night. You need to be receptive to love by cultivating a romantic spirit within yourself, for yourself. Then if/when someone comes along one day— it is simply a matter of sharing that spirit with him or her and receiving from their own romantic spirit, as well. Now this is very important. You need to cultivate your garden of roses for yourself and be willing to share that when someone comes along so that they can smell the fragrance of your roses and help you water them and care for them and possibly bring new species of them to introduce within the walls of your greenhouse. But you need to always know that the garden and the roses are your own creation, that they are there primarily to make you happy and that nobody is allowed to steal them. Someone can add to your garden; but no one can take it away. The idea is that the garden is there before another person arrives, while the person arrives (and it should grow more beautiful with that person there), and it will still be there long after the person is gone (in the event that your paths are not destined to be together for longer.)

Romance is your intention towards life and towards yourself. My mother used to tell me, "If you are buying new clothes and dressing up beautifully and doing your hair beautifully like that— make sure that you are doing all these things because it makes you happy." I think that this is the best advice my mother has ever given me. Of course she taught me this long before my eyes were opened to the true meaning of romance; but perhaps she had planted a mustard seed

inside of me long, long ago. I have always done all of
those things without the thought of any man in mind;
but only with the thought of how it makes *me* feel. But
only now have I seen the truth that there should be no
such thing as loneliness! There should only be journeys
written out, tumbled out, rolled out, woven out! And
loneliness shouldn't be a part of your story because your
story must be a romantic one! You must fill every
crevice of your life with wine and roses.

How To Ride a Horse

When I was much younger, living in a town where my mother managed her own business, she used to raise me based upon the opinions of other people around us. I remember one thing she would frequently say: "Joy, you need to get down from your high horse! You know what people around this town are saying about you? They're saying that you are high and mighty, riding up there on your horse and they can't reach you!"

I already knew myself well at that tender age, well enough to know that it was not as the people were trying to make it look like, it wasn't like that. They were trying to make it look like I was arrogant, that I was proud; but that wasn't the truth and I knew it. I also knew that I did in fact have a horse that I felt like I was always riding on! Perhaps I really was "high" and "mighty" but only due to the fact that I was given a horse and that I was taught how to ride it. They were gifts given to my soul!

"You know, you need to smile more often! You know what people around here are saying? They're saying that you don't look pleasant and sweet!" These were the kinds of remarks I would hear from my mother almost every day. I felt like I had no one on my side because I had to go out into the world and then come home to a place that made me feel like I was still out there in the world! My mom and I weren't a team and

44

that is a very unfortunate detail of my childhood. Perhaps it had something to do with the fact that we don't look the same because I am multiracial while she is bi-racial, leaving me with a quite unique mix that makes me look like I'm not her daughter; or maybe it had something to do with the fact that her and my dad had a very bad breakup. Or it could have been those factors (and possibly more) combined. My mother taught me some very essential, key things in life, which I was very fortunate to receive from her; but I can't honestly say that I had an exemplar childhood that everyone should strive to create for their children, because I didn't! There were multiple factors that were dictating the hardships that I faced growing up as a child, not to mention my own father's battle with drug abuse.

I still held onto the reins of that horse I believed I was given to ride upon! No matter what, and no matter if anybody knew about it, I really did have a horse and, in my opinion, it was okay for me to ride it! I believe that it is okay for us to allow our children to experience the spiritual gifts that they have, to allow them to be who they are! I know that I was a deep thinker and that smiling at everyone in order to "appear pleasing" simply wasn't on my agenda at that time in my life. I was too busy thinking, observing and trying to understand things beyond what the eye can see. I think that it is difficult for some parents to understand the nature of their children/child if those children/that child seems to be different. I believe that us as parents— we must sensitively and actively seek out the signs pointing us to the gifts that our children were born with and to do this means that we need to be active seekers of those things that thrive beyond what the everyday eye can see. We need to see those things around us in our environments as well as inside the eyes of our children. It is okay for them to come into the world as new things that we might not immediately understand or that the world may not ever understand! But we must strive to be their Temples and not only that, but to guide them in the building of themselves as *their own* Temples!

I often hear about the fears that parents have about "spoiling" their children; but True Mystery does not and *cannot* spoil a child. It is through True Mystery that our children are brought back to themselves and there is no self-knowledge that will spoil a person because contrary to what one may think, in the acquiring of the knowledge of the self, the ego is beaten down and slain. And look at what a lie we have been taught by those who would not have us know the truth! We are warned against the perils of "narcissism" and made to believe that the sight of the true self is the well of this; but that is not the truth! It is through the sight of the true self that the ego is laid to waste! It is a demon that we fight on our inward journey and one cannot fight that demon, slay it, but then in the end worship it! The journey into ourselves and the vision pointed inwards is what opens our view to the universe, to the people around us as we see them for who *they* truly are, too! You cannot possibly see others until you have seen yourself and no one can see oneself when selfishness is in the way! Because selfishness will always blind you to whom you truly are, as it does not allow you to see the truths of your nature and your reflection. Selfishness cannot afford to allow you onto your inward journey to know thyself, because on that inward journey you will find glorified monsters on pedestals that you will need to wrestle and beat down. And that is precisely why, as much as possible, selfishness will tell you that everything is fine and perfect in your world, which is actually what deflects you from peering any further into the depth of your own soul. Now isn't this all a rather beautiful quantum irony? It is in fact freedom and courage who will take you by the hand and lead you onto the breathtaking beginning of yourself.

The Pack

I always tell my son that we are "a pack." Like a wolf pack. And that is what he has come to relate our family unit to. I don't try to push the idea that I am his "friend" or that we are "buddies"; but I instill the belief that our family unit is a "pack", not much unlike a wolf pack. We roam the Earth together, we are here because the other is here, we are bonded together, we can howl at the Moon together! What is ours is ours and we protect our own. We're not something that others can easily infiltrate or meddle with. We won't let one another be taken down or picked apart. We don't learn about each other from anyone on the outside; but we learn about each other together, face-to-face and we learn our life lessons together, side-by-side!

I can see that the reason why many young people in the world today would rather be outside of the home and would rather trust other people outside of the family, is because they feel like outside of the home, out there with their friends, they have a "pack" that they belong to. They are not judged, but understood. They don't feel hurried and rushed, but they feel like time stops and all that abounds is laughter and good times. And when bad times do come along, they don't fall apart; they rough it together! Too many children and young adults today form packs outside of the family unit and that is just not in accordance with the ways of the wolf!

Wolves, once a family, are always a family— come what may! The Earth is theirs to roam and the Moon is theirs to love and to fondle! It's all about the pack— everything is!

When us as parents, when we think about "family", what are we really referring to? What do we want our children to expect from that and what kind of definition do we give to our children to understand and to live by? When you were a child or a teenager, what did you want your family to feel like? Because you can still have that, because you can still make that, no matter how long ago it was when you dreamt of what it would be like to have this and to have that.

A family needs each other, to roam the Earth with, to run in the night with, to keep each other warm, to laugh with and to hold, come what may! Family is eternal; but you have to *make* it eternal. You have to live in a bond with your child/children that leaks out the aroma of eternity, a bond that makes them feel so animalistic and so safe and so free all at the same time that they are able to feel in their hearts, that you are indeed a pack. You are your own pack and nothing in the world can ever change that. Not even the things beyond this world can change it. You're not just things that happened to one another; but you are parts of each other's Divine Plan! It is not simply by chance that you came to be flesh and blood (or heart and heart) but it is by chance and by sovereignty and by divine intervention.

Silken Threads

When I arrived in Norway a few years ago, in the city of Drammen, I found myself asking why I was there. Drammen is a beautiful city and Norway is an exceptional country, but I felt like there was nothing for me there. It was too quiet, you couldn't hear people laughing, you couldn't see children in the streets or see people kissing on benches. Norway is picturesque— there are graceful swans that glide along Drammenselva River, swans so perfect that you will not be able to distinguish between reality and fantasy! They reminded me of my grandmother's porcelain swan sculptures that would glide around on a small glass tablet every time I turned on the music (something like a musical snow globe or a jewellery music box). The houses and the flowers, the lawns, the grass, the crystalline pools of water in people's backyards... it was all so perfect. And yet I kept on telling everyone that I didn't belong there! I was staying with family there and though I expressed gratitude for the wonderful hospitality they were showing me, I also didn't hesitate to give them a piece of my mind— Norway was too quiet, the people were all too aloof and unhappy and this just wasn't my kind of city! Especially because I had just come to Norway from Rome! Rome, of all places! The Eternal City of laughter, kissing, gelato and mini scooters! I wanted to go back to "my" city and I often found that I was feeling lonely and cold in Norway. Literally cold! Even in the summertime, Norway can freeze your toes and fingers off!

I met a new friend while I was there, her name is Hege Bjerknes and she is an author, as well! She was renting the second floor of my sister's house and while my sister and her husband were at work, I spent time with Hege, we walked around Drammen, we visited the nearby public garden and took pictures of swans, lilacs and peafowls! I even met a guy in that garden, a guy who was so shy I think he thought I was crazy for talking to him, or worse, he probably thought I was attracted to him! Anyway, on my walks with Hege through Drammen, I went about life as I normally do— taking large amounts of joy from the sensation of biting into strawberries, pointing out magic in rose bushes and shadows on swing sets. I pointed at so many beautiful things that Hege said she hadn't even seen before! Things in her own neighborhood that she hadn't even noticed during all her many years of living there! Even my sister didn't even know that there was an enchanted garden beside the river, only a twenty minute walk from her home, she found out because I took pictures while Hege and I were there and I showed those pictures to her later in the day when she got home from work! To my surprise, I had discovered things in my new surroundings that went unnoticed by the residents of that place, for years! For decades! For their whole lives!

I continued to voice my complaints about Norway the whole time I was there. It's not that I didn't appreciate the beauty of the people or the country; but it's more that I missed Rome, I missed listening to people laugh and seeing people kiss! I missed the air of Rome saturated in the tincture of life itself! I missed the basilica bells... I missed it all and I felt like Norway was on a different planet! People in Norway can't be found on their porches, it is like a beautiful, manicured ghost town! A picture-perfect land inhabited by ghosts! Well, that is how I felt at the time, towards my experience there.

I also continued to enjoy my time with my newfound friends and with my family there. We spent time together listening to a radio station I couldn't understand, we took a tram ride into Drammen City centre, I went window shopping together with my sister and my little niece, Rebecca and I took my little nephew Daniel for walks in his stroller while I ate ice cream in cones along with their grandfather whilst standing under a tree and freezing! And I rolled up tobacco with Hege so we could smoke by the river (a very needful thing to do in such cold Norwegian weather.) So as you can see, during my time in Drammen, I made connections and I created moments that I wasn't even aware of. While I was busy thinking about how much I wanted to go back to Rome, I was inevitably creating something beautiful right there where I was, a world away from where I wanted to be!

A day before my departure back to Rome, Hege gave me a handmade greeting card with her heartfelt message for me, which read, "You showed me stars I didn't know... I will remember you so brave and all the brightening that you gave." Also, my niece and nephew's grandfather hugged me and told me, "I am happy and my world is new because you are now here in it." And I must point out, that Norwegians don't just say things to be nice, because they are not particularly concerned with trying to show people that they are happy and nice, they would rather stick to their own and mind their own business (but that is not to say that they are not kind people), so receiving these words from the two Norwegian people that had made entrance into my life without my even noticing it very much, really touched me at my core. It gripped me at the heart of myself and it shook me by the shoulders, waking me up to a whole new and vibrant truth! It is there that I learned one of the most important things to know in this life! It is there that I learned that things are not just about us and our own happiness or just about us and what we want! My journey to Norway wasn't about me; it was about other people!

We can go around in life looking for happiness in every nook and cranny, looking for fulfillment, trying to "find ourselves", trying to believe in new things and striving to be raptured by new ways of being and new experiences to awaken our senses and remind us of who we really are and what we are here for— and that's all good— but the fundamental beautiful and solemn truth remains, that it is not going to always be about us. It is not going to always be about what we want and what is going to make us happy in the moment or how other people can make us happy; but it is also going to be about us being blessings in other people's lives. It is also about us becoming the experience of a lifetime for other people to have! It is indeed also about us being the stars that someone has never seen before, the world that someone else has never traversed before (or maybe never even heard of before)! We can fill ourselves up with our own senses all too often, without leaving room for the senses of other people, removing from our eyes the ability to see what we are doing for other people in their lives, that we have in fact become miracles for other people, simply by being there! Simply by being ourselves!

And so it wasn't all about me, after all. But the funny thing is, that in it not being all about me at the end of the day, it did in fact become all about me, as a fact. Because at the end of the day, I did learn a priceless lesson that I will forever cherish, I was able to see life through a whole new hue in the whole stained glass window of truth and to top it all off, I made good friends!

Since I have come to know this truth, I want my son to know it and I want you to know it and I want your sons and daughters to know it, I want us all to see that sometimes we are not just the receivers of a beautiful world; but sometimes, we are creators of new worlds for other people and we might not even know it. We must possess ourselves and seize ourselves in such a way that we are able to have a keen eye for seeing just when we have become a miracle, so that we can stop being disappointed in our whereabouts, so we can stop being disappointed that we are in quiet Norway when we want to be in boisterous Rome. We must cultivate in our children the ability to realize when they have in fact become stars in other people's skies and new worlds in other people's hearts. And I am not even talking about the desire to be an inspiration or the desire to "be the change" nor any of those popular slogans that we are all "supposed" to be living by, I'm not even referring to those, not in the least! But I am in fact referring to an ability to see the hand of God, the hands of the Gods, the hand of providence and sovereignty, as we are embroidered into a tapestry not only to be receiver of all the compliments of admirers who will eventually come along to admire the handmade piece; but we are also destined to become the fabrics that give a reason for the rest of the piece to be beautiful, too. And that, at the end of the day, only means one in the same thing! Both fabrics are beautiful, both fabrics draw attention to their silken fibers and the way that they catch the sunlight (and an admiring eye). The fabric that is there to receive of the tincture of the beautiful world is no less fortunate than the fabric woven in order to make the whole tapestry beautiful to look at, in order to make all the other fabrics resplendent just by being where they are, beside the other one. In fact, when looking at the tapestry, you will only see a whole piece of interwoven silken threads and the amazing thing here is that we are all both types of threads! Both the one to receive and the one to give! When all is said and done, giving and receiving are both the same thing! And that is why Hege will always remember me, even if at the time I didn't even really want to be there.

It is a great and admirable feat to cultivate the nature of being able to feed off of the tinctures that the world has to offer; but it is altogether a magnanimous thing, to actually become one of those tinctures.

Disclaimer: I only "roll up tobacco" in Drammen (which is not very often.)

Wise as the Serpents

I always tell my son, "Don't be like the people who don't know what to do with the tools that are given to them."

There are so many tools that we are given, in every situation we are in and in every place that we go to— there are lessons to be had, even in the seemingly smallest things that happen to us— we must learn from them. Time and time again, I watch learning opportunities pass under people's noses without them seeing the relevance of the occurrence to their position in life and I believe this is because people have lost the ability to see the Hands of Divine Intervention within the seemingly mundane "coincidences" in life. But nothing is a coincidence for the student of magic, nothing is a coincidence for those whom are chosen, each person that comes along, each thing that we observe— all of these things work together to teach us something, to develop our intuition, foresight and perception! And by the gaining of more perception we are led to perceiving even more and so on and so forth. Happenings in your life must not fall on deaf ears and blind eyes. There are quite a few instances wherein I knew that I had "occurred" in a person's life for a divine purpose and yet I had to stand by and watch the person being painfully oblivious to any purpose in my arrival, or anything whatsoever! Unfortunately, many people are void of the skill of seeing the significance in circumstances, situations, happenings, chances and other people. How does this happen? It happens when the soul of a person falls into a numbness, a sleep. It happens as a result of losing Divine Eyesight. Or rather, it was never even there to begin with! People deny the soft nudges of things that take place in their day-to-day lives and of people that come along their paths, because they have developed a certain kind of sense of entitlement that dictates everyone and everything needs to come with a weight of proof in order to be believed. People want to sit down and let things and people prove themselves to them. People actually enjoy being blind! They're afraid of being laughed at, of being mocked for believing in magic and so they repel magic from their lives so even when magic does happen to them, they are too afraid to see those things for what they are! Or maybe, they are simply incapable of the task, entirely.

In the children's tale, *The Emperor's New Clothes* by Hans Christian Andersen, there was only one boy who was brave and true enough to point out that the Emperor was in fact naked. Everybody else, even the Emperor himself, were all too afraid of being seen as fools so while everyone pretended to behold the "lovely robes" that supposedly draped the Emperor's body, out of fear of being called fools because they could not see the "special" kind of cloth that could only be seen by the wise— the Emperor was in fact naked— and there was but a single person in the entire kingdom (a young boy) who was true enough to just say, "Hey! The Emperor is naked!" I believe that this children's tale is an accurate depiction of what goes on today and sadly, the ratio of the seeing ones to the blind ones is depicted quite accurately, as well! Oh how few people I have met in my life whom I can truly say I believe to be brave, honest and awake! *Everyone* is too afraid of being called a fool for being able to see what is natural and by natural, you know that I mean supernatural. Because what is supernatural is only natural and it is only for fear of being called foolish that people turn away from these things. People cannot see significance and they allow immensely valuable lessons and other people to come in and out of their lives without even taking anything from those gifts that are given to them! All that significance *is* the natural state of things and people are blinded by the prospect of embarrassment, which is why they would rather exist and go about their business like all of those other characters in the tale of *The Emperor's New Clothes*. They would rather live in an unnatural state and fool themselves, instead of risking the fact of being called a fool by others. There are two kinds of people: one that for fear of being called a fool, will shy away from magic, and the other, for sheer disgust of appearing foolish in his/her own eyes, cannot fathom fooling his/her self only to appease popular opinion.

Nothing and nobody carries the burden of proof in our presence. Things and people don't carry the burden of proving themselves to us and it is we who must strive to be keen, to be spiritually cunning, learning to grasp what comes our way and wield those things into tools for us in our lives for our growth and development.

The other day, I opened the front door of our home to see what would happen to the stray cat whom I have been feeding since she was just a kitten (I guess that might mean that she isn't actually a stray anymore), when she saw the front door open for her. This particular cat is the offspring of a stray that came along, whom I named "Alessandra." So I opened the door to see if she would like to take a stroll around the house and sure enough, she cautiously strode inside the living room, looking around curiously. I closed the door just to keep the mosquitoes out and that's when the cat went ballistic! She became so disoriented with her surroundings simply because one thing changed and possibly made her feel insecure, that she began running around the living room, frantically meowing and clawing at the curtains! She even ran straight into the glass door which was *right beside* the door that she came in through, which I had reopened the minute I realized she was disoriented and was about to lose it! I didn't open the glass door because it was being kept close for repair issues. I kept on standing in the open front door, showing her the way, I kept on calling out to her to make her see that the door was open again! She just couldn't see it! She would rather race into the door right beside the open one, banging her head on it, only to make herself even more panicky until finally, after totally losing it, she found a corner to hide in. She wouldn't let me near her, either! She hissed and tried to scratch me when I went to her in the corner with some pieces of fish to lure her out. I needed to think fast because my son's grandparents were paying a visit and they don't appreciate cats (especially stray ones), so what I did was I placed the pieces of fish in the open doorway, at an angle where the cat could see it from where she was hiding, then I called her mother in to eat the fish and there she saw her mother and jumped out of hiding as if she had been in horrific exile for days!

Now, what happened to the cat left an impression upon me, but I didn't realize that the very next day I would be applying what I had learned/seen, to my own life! Twenty-four hours later and I found myself in a situation with my manuscripts. I needed to edit some of my manuscripts' contents, so I edited the PDF's and resubmitted them for publishing, only to get word back from the publishing warehouse, saying that the specifications of my PDF were not acceptable for printing. I began to panic and I felt angry, too. I only made very minor edits, only to polish them up even more, then out of the blue the warehouse wouldn't accept them? Suddenly there was an unexpected change that made me feel disoriented and insecure about the future of these manuscripts that I had pulled out just for some very minor editing! I began to panic so badly that I started concocting all possible scenarios in my mind and theoretically running myself through each of those possible scenarios! That's when I remembered the cat, because I was acting just like her. That's when I realized that the door was probably open and I just couldn't see it. I decided to place my trust in the Divine Hands and believe that there was no need to fling myself into such discomfort merely as a reaction to momentary insecurity. And then I even went so far as to say to myself, "Oh well, if these two books don't ever make it through, I still have six others on the shelves, with a new one on the way!"

Things happen to us like gifts served up to our consciousness, in order for us to use them as tools for our own souls, for our own being! I don't think that everyone would have been able to see the connection between what happened to the cat and what happened to me the very next day; but I did! But beyond myself, I would like to see my son being able to do the same, I would like to see him being able to extract from the tincture of people and of things (anything that happens), in order to use each as a tool for his betterment, for his learning, development and ultimately his formation. I would also like to see the same in you and in your own children. I do not want to observe an entire race of individuals walking around as if living in the pages of *The Emperor's New Clothes.* Sure, some know-it-all, if he or she had seen it all, might have said to me, "You're crazy, I don't see anything there!" but I know that I would rather not fool myself than be preoccupied with not appearing foolish to another!

There are all these tools that are given to us in life and that includes the development of our own talents, ideas and strengths. To "seize the day" is not just a passing slogan and in fact, it's more like, "seize the moment!" Because moments can come and go unnoticed right beneath our noses and if we are not cunning enough and true enough, we aren't going to be able to seize the tincture of them. There are messages brought to us in dreams, there are signs that are revealed to us through our dreams at night and yet most people dismiss these things as "mere fantasy" in the morning. Let me tell you this, that the majority of things I have learned and have written about, which are quoted by people the world over and believed by them to have changed their lives and set them on new paths— those things were revealed to me in my dreams at night! Think about that. I have readers who are astronauts and therapists and world-renowned psychologists, multi-award winning scientists, who subscribe to my thoughts and where have these thoughts come from? They are recognized as truth but where do they come from? They come from whispers, nudges and they come from experiences given to me in my dreams at night! Now what would happen if I were to wake up in the morning and dismiss those signs and wonders as mere fantasies constructed by my brain during slips through different levels of consciousness? Well I'll tell you what would happen: I wouldn't be writing those things, I wouldn't be writing this book and you probably wouldn't even know that I exist!

There are children who come into the world born with the keenness to catch the significance in the signs that are given to them, but unfortunately, too often the noise of the world shuts that out, tells them that what they know is a lie. There are children brought into the world who see the higher vibrational aspects of everything, who are able to tap into that and communicate with that and even to speak that language to others. Don't shut them out, don't shut them down. I remember the era in my life when I was shut down and out, when I look back at that period not so long ago, I see a dull individual who was just existing, not really seeing or understanding any purpose! Don't be like most people, don't sit there with an array of gifts in front of you, being too incapable of even picking them up! Don't feel entitled, and always be sure to call a naked Emperor, naked!

A Very Short Discourse on Magic

Magic is the ancient flame, the true religion, the original spirituality, the original fire. If you search for spirituality from long ago— what you will find is magic! You won't find manuscripts about religion like today; but you will find manuscripts of magic. Even if we look at the story of the birth of Christ, we will see, that it was the Magi who brought the Christ precious gifts, it was they who predicted his birth by reading the skies (astrology) and it was they who found him. Who are the Magi? The Magi are of the original lineage of what we now call The Rosicrucians. What and who are these people? These people are the keepers of esoteric secrets— THE laws of nature. And I say "nature" instead of "supernature" because magic is actually the supernatural *knowledge* of what is simply natural. To see what is natural with eyes uncovered, to see what is natural with supernatural eyes— is to see magic!

I suppose they began burning certain peoples at the stake in order to eliminate the magical bloodlines. Some would argue that these bloodlines come straight from Angelic decent (from the time when Angels mated with women.) And sometimes I stop to ask myself *why destroy them?* But then in a split second I realize that the answer to that question is so simple! A magical race could not be controlled! Could not be overpowered! Whoever was to come into power would need to subdue

such people.

Long before there was religion, there was magic. And wherever we look into the past, back at the roots of this ancient flame, we will find propaganda against it. Black propaganda trying to make us believe that the magical were baby killers and murderers who sacrificed innocent lives on altars! This is so far from the truth; the truth is far detached from what we are told. It is religion that has murdered all throughout history and these are known facts; not just stories pieced together by archeologists deciphering drawings on stones. I can imagine that if religion had not come in to subdue the magical, today we would probably look like those places we now like to call "Middle Earth." And I find that hypothetical place to be more appealing than the skyscrapers and the wars that we have today.

I am a woman of science. I study astronomy as well as the sciences of life, politics, animals and food... where there is something to learn— there you can find me! But what I have learned is that science is inferior to magic. What we think we know today in science— ten years from now we prove as wrong! We only *think* we know these things; we *think* we know facts, but the truth is that all we really know are the names we have ourselves given to things! We observe things, *as they already are*, these natural laws that have already been around since the time before we were born! Before the "father of the atom" named the thing as an "atom", the atom was already there! No person conjured the atom into existence! The atom does not belong to any scientist! It just so happens that someone named it so. And so the scientist goes through life naming things in order to tell a story. And what story is this? It is the story of why and how things are the way they are. It is just like religion. Science and religion strive to do the same thing; the difference is that the two speak an entirely different language! One of numbers, algorithms, equations; the other of parables, legends, ballads and song! Both desire to explain nature, the laws of the universe and the governing traits that dictate why your life is useful. Both are beautiful and essential in their own ways but they cannot compare to the Original Flame.

Magic is the same yesterday, as it is today. The magic of thousands and thousands of years ago is no less potent today, is not disproved today! It is the same yesterday, today and forever. And this is why I put my trust in magic.

Dear Dying Race,

People today do not understand the meaning of sacrifice. In fact, you might not even want to read the rest of what I have written here, after reading the word "sacrifice" in the first sentence. This word has become synonymous with religion and with loss. The majority of modern society believes that sacrifice is the ultimate loss and has completely failed to associate it with any sort of gain, whatsoever!

The sad part is how children these days are not raised; they are just born and then they are "raised" by the media: television, movies, magazines, Facebook, popular opinion, popular culture... their convictions are just about as deep as the width of a magazine spread of the latest supermodel! And when I say "children" you'd be surprised to realize that I am pertaining not only to our younger generation but also to my own generation because I see even my own generation as "children." Then these children are "raised" by the media inside the illusion that they should expect only the best out of every single thing that comes their way and that any form of discomfort on their part is to be shunned and feared; of course, this illusion is only created by advertising teams of companies that want you to buy their products. The message is coming from the left and from the right of people's Facebook accounts, from televisions, from the magazines, from internet blog articles and so on and so forth— the message that their product will make you *feel better* and give you better than the next product can— the sickening illusion that the world is catering to you and trying to give you all the things that will make you feel good! People sit there and buy into this illusion, expecting that their lives are supposed to work that way, expecting that this is what it's supposed to feel like, expecting total comfort as a sign of quality and happiness... people are stupid! Meanwhile, the reality is merely that companies are trying to make money so that their CEO can live in utter comfort. That's the reality.

The reality of sacrifice in life is both a scientific and fundamental spiritual and moral reality. In order to accept a new energy, one must sacrifice another energy to make room for the new one. In order to accept something that you want— you have to be able to see its value and prioritize it above something else. Energies are not equal. People's energies are not equal, the energies added to your life by other people and by activities and decisions and choices— they are not equal! *The key skill that needs to be cultivated in one's life is the ability to assess value.* Unfortunately, this ability is often crushed underfoot by the stupidity created by the hands of the aforementioned rhythm of current society. How can an individual assess the value of a person or a thing in order to prioritize and build a beautiful life around or with it, when that same individual assesses the value of *everything* based upon how he/she was "raised" by the media? Based upon magazine spreads and advertisements? Based upon how many Facebook "likes" something gets? My God!

In order to be a good husband and have a happy family, a man must assess the value of having a wife as greater than the value of having a fuckbuddy. In order to be a good wife and mother, a woman must be capable of assessing the value of her children over the value of her career and the value of her husband over the value of a fling. The stupidity unfolds when people exhibit no abilities whatsoever to see the varying values of people, circumstances, choices, decisions and things! And the frightening fact is that this special kind of stupid is all the rage! This truly frightens me. It frightens me to realize that it is possible to marry a person who does not see a difference of worth between the person he/she is marrying and the person whom he/she used to fuck for the weekend! It frightens me to realize that a mother may not be able to assess the value of her child as greater than the value of her waistline! And one may argue that it is all about what one values in life; but this is a falsity. There are universal values designated to things and to people and those do not change based upon what you choose to think! The value of your child will *always* be greater than the value of your waistline or the value of your job! The value of the children of a nation will *always* be greater than the value of that nation's corporate makeup and political landscape! Even if the values change in the minds of the people and the children become fifth in line or the family becomes tenth in line; the only outcome of that is distress, imbalance and rot! The values of the things do not actually change; what changes is the quality of people's purpose and lives! People begin to lose in life. They begin to "win" in what they *think* is what's worth winning in; but then they lose in life! And the thing is that they know it! They know it in their hearts! There is an emptiness, a loss, a never-ending fall that just keeps on going down, down, down and they try to fill it up but it just doesn't get filled up! This is because we do not designate the value of things. The value of a thing is set as eternity is set. *You* are more valuable than the world and everything in it, simply because God gave you that value and this doesn't change throughout time or throughout lifetimes! No matter how the world system seeks to make the person as second best to the corporate, to the company, to the systems making money— all the systems rot in the end, as a result of this imbalance! Because the person is of more value and yet a system is placing more value upon itself than upon the individuals! In the end we see crises, we see destitution, we see unanswered questions and unsolved problems.

There is always a sacrifice made in order to solidify the worth of something. Sacrifice is what gives anything its worth; whether it was a sacrifice made by another for all of mankind on a cross a long time ago or if it was a sacrifice made by a nation or by a certain people or by a single person for his lover or for his friend! Sacrifice is an act that gives merit and gives value to something else that is worth that merit and that is worth that value. The fact that the generation of today does not recognize this (and I'm including my own generation here) is testament to the reality of this dying race. Of this stupid people.

Sacrifice something in order to let something else in. Know the value of things by seeing their purpose, their meaning and their depth! Create something for your future by living to be that kind of person *now*. Things are not advertisements, people are not advertisements— they do not exist for our comfort or for our pleasure! Furthermore, how do you measure pleasure in your person? Do you measure your pleasure by the experience of things that are easily coming and easily going or do you measure your experience of pleasure in things that are lasting? And the question furthermore expands to ask, "Do you know how to make lasting things? And do you know how to make things last? Do you know how to place value in a thing, in a choice, circumstance or decision, in a way that makes it a lasting thing? And by what means can we create such a value to place into something or someone?" This value is created by the means of a strong willpower. The Will of man must be the King of all his person— body, soul and spirit. It is the strong Will of man that is able to create and to project and to make anything take root whatsoever it desires. But this Will is cultivated not against the natures that be; but in accordance to the natures that be. And what are these natures? These natures are the laws that are called "supernatural" by those who know not of its ways! But the truth is that what is supernatural to them is simply called "natural."

What is supernatural to you is only natural to me. We have the supernatural knowledge of what is natural and in this the Will must be cultivated. You cultivate your Will by believing in things before they are seen, by creating things out of nothing, by *willing* what is meant to be— into being! It is the Will of man and woman that reaches far above the illusions of this stupid society we are all trapped in and what's more, reaches so far and above that we are no longer trapped underneath that stupidity! All sparks are created by the friction made when what is natural fights to escape what is unnatural (keep in mind the true meaning of natural and unnatural.) All the unnatural shit that you're supposed to believe is more important than having a family, than being a mother, than loving someone— *that's* your bondage, that's your trap! And the funniest part of all this is how you actually believe that your trap is your freedom! But then isn't that how all traps keep you there inside of them? By making you feel like they are your freedom?

Mistakes

Lately, I have been thinking about society's attitude towards mistakes. I've recently said that the world will tell us over and over again that mistakes are always good and I myself have once said, "So what? This is life! A whole bunch of mistakes!" Nevertheless, I do feel that when this creed falls upon a ground that has not yet been tilled, it creates stupidity. Yes, we are free to make mistakes but on the other hand we are also free to choose the experiences that we allow to take root into our lives or to even become a part of our lives, in the first place. The thing is, once a mistake is made, you will have to live with the consequences of those actions that are most probably going to be far-reaching and will touch not only your life but also the lives of those whom you love. I frequently hear many people say, "I would not do anything differently, I would not have done anything any other way." I personally do not say that. There are plenty of things I would have done differently and the fact that I can see that and I realize that, means that I have learned from mistakes made. I am thankful for the things learned; but I am not glad that the errors were made, especially in circumstances where I have hurt other people. I believe that in any circumstance where you have hurt another person, the right to say, "I wouldn't have done anything any other way" isn't a right that belongs to you, because your actions have involved hurting another person/ other people! It's easy for you to say but what about the other person or the other people that you hurt? In fact, when I come to see my mistakes and see where I went wrong, or how bad I was, I feel a true joy and gratitude for being able to see the error in my ways. It brings me joy and gratitude because those errors were chains that bound me. When you are not able to see those chains or refuse to acknowledge that they are there— you fail to be freed of them!

There is an immense lack of responsibility that exists in society today. I am glad that people are being taught their worth and importance and that they are "the universe" but dare I say that these teachings, when fallen into the hands of the unperceiving, create nothing but an empty sense of self-entitlement and lack of responsibility for one's own actions? The hierophants of ancient days were earnest in giving the warning that certain knowledge not be given to the masses without proper introduction and inner growth. The raw fact is that not all people are ready to know certain truths. There is a reason why such truths are kept away. When fallen into the hands of the unprepared— there is no good outcome.

Worth is a word that many people do not have a true grasp of. It is very important to understand that your quality and your worth do not make you numb and blind to the consequences of your own actions. In fact, our worth is increased by seeing the faults of our own ways! The faults of your ways are like dried cow dung stuck all over a mesmerizing mermaid's tail! And I know that is a rather strange example but it is the first thing that came to mind! So imagine having a mermaid with dried cow dung stuck all over her tail— you want to wash all of that diseased, offensive stuff away, you don't need to be saying, "Oh I am proud of all that poop all over this mermaid's tail." You can just be humble and wash all of that poop away. But first you have to see it and identify it as such. The fact is that it takes humility to see and to identify the things that we ought to not have done and the people we ought to not have hurt. Change comes from humility and we all want to change, to grow, to become. Whenever I see mistakes in me and faults in me— I rejoice! I truly do and the reason why I do that is because I just feel so joyous about knowing that my eyes have been opened, my consciousness raised! The poop that I see on my mermaid's tail is the poop that I can get rid of to reveal a vibrant variety of iridescent, opalescent colours underneath!

Seize!

We watch the heroes in movies get chance after chance after chance in their lives. Life is always ripe for the hero in a movie, ripe full of chances, second chances, third chances, until in the end they emerge victorious!

We are the heroes of our own lives, the stars of our own movies. Our realities are like movies for the gods and the angels and we star in them. However, in reality, we don't always get second chances, third chances, and an unending number of chances! That's just not how it works in real life. In our lives, sometimes we only get one chance at a wonderful thing and if we don't take that first chance we'll never get it back again, or we'll never get another one just like it. Life is tough like that. We have all these paths in front of us and to our right and to our left, making each choice that we make into a pathway towards a product distinctly different from the others around it. Whenever we don't do something, that is actually a choice not to do something and a choice not to do something isn't nothing; rather, it is another path taken. So rare is a path that duplicates the product or duplicates the scenery or the pavement of itself! The chances that we do get are unique and rare.

There are big chances and there are small chances. There are life-changing chances and then there are the everyday choices that we make, steps that we take towards our own happiness, or towards the happiness of our loved ones, or towards the betterment of our craft or our hobbies. And while the small choices that we make and the small chances that we get are very precious; it's the big chances that come along which take our breath away and capture our memories forever! We get big chances to learn something, to change some deeply seated flaws, to change the world! But often, we're too comfortable where we are, we're too afraid, we're unsure of ourselves or of God, we're complacent, we're satisfied, we're too virtuous or we're too dumb to take them! Or we think that because we are the authors of our own stories, the heroes and heroines of our own lives, the protagonists of our very own novels, that must mean everything will work out in the end for our own good and that means if we don't do something now we can always do it later. But that is how we keep on messing up. Because in real life, nobody is going to keep on waiting for us to get ready, nobody is going to keep on waiting for us to get on the train or to say hello or to smile at them on the sidewalk. Nobody is going to keep on waiting for us to abandon what we have known as truth in search of our own truth! But we have to do that, *you* have to do that! And sometimes, even when you're supposed to take centre stage at a particular scene in your life, you end up being the spectator when your own role is given to someone else who is competent enough, who is ready, who is willing and who is able.

When I was just a young child in kindergarten, I remember very vividly how I was supposed to be the star runner of my class as well as the star reader. But I was too afraid of the attention, too embarrassed by the thought of everyone looking at me and wondering why I could run so fast, wondering why I could read so well! The thought terrified me! I didn't want anyone to see me as different, I didn't want to stand out, I didn't want anybody staring at me or wondering why and whispering amongst themselves about how I was different. I didn't want to excel, I didn't want to be better and I didn't want to shine! So instead of being the star runner, I purposefully lagged behind and ran just fast enough (slow) to be alongside everyone else on the track. And instead of being the star reader at the graduation ceremonies, since I refused to take that position, it was then given to the next best reader in class who was delighted to fill in my shoes! Meanwhile, I ended up becoming a plush vegetable decorating the stage in the background and I was just fine with that! I was contented to be the overgrown stuffed vegetable decorating the theatre stage whilst my teacher, Mrs. Sergeant, stared at me like I was crazy in the head! But that's not where the story ends; that's just how it began!

After kindergarten, I was given plenty of chances to shine and I reacted the same way each time, just as I did back when I was in K-5. As if I had all the chances in the world! But guess what! Later in my life things changed and oh how I wished I could turn back time! Oh God knows just how much I wished I could turn back time! *If only, if only, if only* I could have gone back to change the choices that I made in the past! And here's the big lesson that I learned from this: that even though

I was just in kindergarten, just a small child, it didn't mean that life would take pity on me! Life didn't say, "Let's change her mind and thus alter the course of many similar mistakes in the future!" No, nothing like that happened! Life let it be all up to me! Life is simply not merciful towards those who do not seize the day, the hour, the moment.

When we know that we are loved from Above, it is easier for us to dwell on that feeling instead of seizing the opportunities presented by it! Unfortunately, that is the very reason why we come upon pitfalls that leave us feeling abandoned by God and all other forms of spiritual aide! Because when this cushion is removed from under us, that is when we begin to see the need to seize the beauties that are placed into the palms of our hands! Beauties that should have been seized previously, beauties that should have been bitten into and chewed on before! We remember the sweetness of honey when all the bees have died, and this is something most unfortunate.

But honey can be our food even while the bees live, even while the flowers still bloom and even while there is still milk flowing in the land! We can feast upon the honey, pick the flowers and drink of the milk! We really don't have to wait to learn this lesson the hard way. I used to always prefer learning things the hard way because I thought the hard way was *my* way; until I learned and realized that I shouldn't want my way to be hard! Why would I want any way that is my own to be hard? Why couldn't my way be easy? Why couldn't my way be laden with rose petals? So it took me a very long time before I saw the truth that I needed to thrive in the land of milk and honey within my own mind and within my own soul, without ever waiting for it to run bitter and dry before beginning to plant seeds and to shine like the Sun that brings those seeds their life! It took me a very long time but I have now learned to be a graceful receiver of favour and to cherish any beauties that are given to me by destiny, whilst choosing to thrive in them and choosing to wield them as a master craftsman, a master builder and creator.

Let us remember that life takes no pity upon us regardless of age or lot in life! Life waits for no one! So when you are loved, when you hold beauties in your hands, you *must* know it! And you must be ready to be the hero/heroine of your own life. Be ready as who and what you are, when you are it.

Alchemical Treatise

Alchemy, according to Merriam-Webster, is "a science that was used in the Middle Ages with the goal of changing ordinary metals into gold" and, "a power or process of transforming something common into something special". Talked about often in 15'th century manuscripts, is, "the alchemy of the soul." And really, physical alchemy is the corporeal existence of the alchemy of the soul, which is the incorporeal side of it. To take a common soul and to transmutate it into what it originally was. Imagine that. And in some cases, to transmutate it into more than what it originally was (as we can see in the case of Enoch becoming Metatron.)

The basic principle of all magic is transmutation. In this world, we are given all manner of vile materials to build our existence with. We are given mud and hatred, excrement and vengeance; we are given broken clay jars and jagged wounds. We are given shards of what once was, we are given anger and envy! Soul Science/Soul Alchemy, is the very difficult process of transmutating those materials that this corporeal world gives us, that our corporeal bodies give to us, into materials pure and sacred, into materials pristine and beautiful for our use in the building of ourselves and our lives. We can turn fault-finding into understanding, we can turn hatred into forgiveness, we can turn anger into love, into acceptance. And I am not talking about a religious perspective or the perspective of "shedding positivity into the Universe" or any of the more popular, well-known methodologies abundant in the world right now; but I am talking about a specific science of the soul. I am talking about specific alchemy of the soul. I am talking about directly taking the negative materials and actively transmutating them into their positive equivalents. Taking an excrement on the ground into your hands and with your palm and your fingers— transforming it into a peach tree!

The deveopment of magical skills comes about due to friction; all development of the initiate is sharpened, grown and honed through the process of friction. For example, during archaic and medieval times, an exercise to develop the Aeth (Aether/Ether) within oneself, was to allow oneself to feel such great an anger towards one's enemy, up to the point that the blood in the body boils (so to speak) and the urge to break a table in half with an axe is so overwhelming, or the urge to wring the other person's neck is so strong that it seethes right below the surface of the skin; then upon reaching this point of utmost anger— to then introduce "the controlling of the fire with the water" which is the process of taming that same material one has allowed to build up to boiling points. One would, during this process of "water bending", produce soothing, comforting thoughts, convincing onself of his/her wrong judgment of the subject in question (the enemy). One would produce, control and direct those soothing waters to put out the flames of fire one had produced and fanned into monstrous proportions just earlier. This friction, this production of fire and water, was a basic training technique utilized in order to produce most absolute magical powers, in order to chisel away at the structure of the soul, to form a perfected one (a perfected soul form.)

In our lives, we are provided with various and inumerable means and opportunities for us to waterbend. There are many instances of flames and fires bursting into existence, wherein we may exercise the craft of waterbending. In fact, I believe that this is the very same craft that Christ of the Bible was referring to when He urged His followers to, "pray for those who despitefully use you", to give a bread to those who would throw stones at you, to turn your other cheek to anyone who would slap you... the world and the church has since interpreted it as a meekness; when in fact, in the secret schools of ancient magic, Christ of the Bible was amongst the most revered, if not *the* most revered, of Masters of the Art. Christ was an initiate, an adept, a Magi, a Master of the Soul, the Son of God. Later on, when Christ's story was picked up by people and formed into a religion that we now know as Christianity, the true messages were scewered in order to look like something else, in order to look like something not magical. But in actuality, Christ was teaching, is teaching us, the most basic and effective way of Soul Development. It is not a meekness; it is an active pursuit of the Aeth!

The most productive way to work with friction for one's benefit, is to take control of the fire as well as the water. At first, life gives you fire (or maybe the Ascended Masters are the ones giving you the fire, aiding in your development) but later on you may produce this fire at your own will, as described earlier. So you are actually consciously excercising two arts: the art of waterbending *and* the art of firebending. The other two elements are already included in this, as both fire and water incorporate the air and the Earth in their compositions and/or ability to thrive. Our human bodies are "the Earth" element in this case, as we can see in the story of our bodies coming from the ground. Hence, during periods of producing fire (anger, hatred, etc.) for purposes of transmutation excercises, you will feel your physical temperature rise, your blood boil. Actually, the story of the creation of man is alluding to this great secret in elemental magic, in the bending of elements. The creation story of the Bible alludes to the fact that the element of Earth that is needed to work with the elements of water and fire, is already present for our souls' use, in the form of our physical bodies. The last element (but not least) being air— well we already all know that air is needed for us to keep staying on this planet. But what about those who are made differently and are not made of the Earth (yes, there are those)? Well for those, there is the Earth all around them, from which their souls may draw upon this particular element.

All gross material may be transmuted into material of fine and pure nature. All of it. The levels of being able to actively practice this transmutation will rely upon the initiate's growth and honing of these skills. This is not something that one half-heartedly may obtain; but this is a great work that is most difficult to perform, requiring all of one's Strengh of Will. For it is really in the excercising of the Strength of Will that the foundation for all the rest of this is laid upon.

The most powerful thing that may be taught to a child, is this art of transmutation. When one has developed the ability to transmutate all negative energy into positive energy, one has possessed the knowledge to transform one's existence and surroundings into what is positive. And this is not a selfish art; because transmutation uses up the dark energy in order to produce the light (the principle of fire itself). We **are not** looking at a craft that ignores what is dark in order to imagine into existence what is light thus producing a race of individuals who only know how to leech onto the light but do not know how to confront and work upon the darkness. What we want to raise are children who are brave enough to face the darkness and capable enough to wield and to transmutate it into what is light. It is not a weakness to stand in front of the darkness and to feel its breath upon the surface of your skin; that is not weakness. It is strength to be able to stand so near in front of darkness and then to transmutate it, transforming it into what is light until such a level is reached that upon touching your own skin, your own breath, your own aura— the darkness is transformed, is transmutated, simply because you are there! Similar is

the principle of courage in that courage is not the
absence of fear but it is performed in the act of
continuing on even in the face of fear. Who wants to
produce a courage that is only imitated and that is not
founded upon an ability to continue on in the face of
fear? So that is not even courage, at all! Are we here to
produce leeches of the light or are we here to produce
warriors of the light?

I worry about the present-day prevailing concept
of "light-leeching." Although I am not going to say that
the whole concept is wrong, simply because it is not my
place to judge this, I will most surely say that I worry
about that mindset and I worry about its whole
movement through societies, everywhere. Is it realistic
to dream after a state of worldwide peace wherein there
are no warriors, no soldiers, no defenders? Is it realistic
to turn a blind eye? Because ever since the beginning of
time itself, there has existed darkness. In fact, from the
darkness was born the first spark of light! We create
light because of the fact that there is initial darkness! So
are they not stripping themselves of reality when they
sit and dream about a state of peace wherein there are no
warriors, no need for soldiers and fighters? Is it realistic
to sit and dream of a state of constant light wherein no
warriors of the light are needed? This, to me, is
unrealistic. This, to me, is the denial of the nature and
the origins of light itself. And what is your real
relationship with light, what real connection can you
ever have with the light, if you do not know its origins?
From darkness was born light; it was not darkness that

C. JoyBell C.

was born from the light! From darkness we become
warriors of the light by ushering it (the light) out of the
darkness. *This is the law of nature.* And so I worry about
the present-day teachings that give counsel on the
premise of ignoring the existence of darkness in hopes of
bringing light into being! Because that is a false pretense
and false pretenses are dangerous! Yes, if you have
reached that level wherein your existence in itself is so
transformative that by your breath and by your presence
alone you are able to decree death unto the darkness and
birth unto a new form of light— in that case— the
darkness will willfully and happily fulfill the destiny
bestowed upon it and will die most fervently at the touch
of your hand, will die most truly at the touch of breath
from your lungs! It is the destiny of darkness to fulfill
and to usher in the light! *Light warriors are we who fulfill
the destiny of darkness and carry the presence of light.* But
this is a level reached after very large amounts of
difficulty; it is not a state that one may imagine or dream
into existence. Teachers do not know this (or perhaps
are ignoring this in favour of making large sums of
money) and as a result, are producing a race of dreamers
and I do not mean that in the beautiful sense of the word
but I mean that in the sense that they are producing a
race of constantly-sleeping souls! They are lulling souls
to sleep!

May we be light warriors, wielding the sceptres of
transformative alchemy skilfully in our hands and may
we bring new souls into this world, teaching them to do
the same.

The Intimacy of Existence

It is in the inner silence of ourselves wherein we will feel and experience our existence; not without, amongst the outer noise. But the outer noise must be a place where we dance freely not because we haven't experienced ourselves in the silence, but because we have first learned to dance on our own.

People can wonder about what freedom is and most of the time they will throw themselves into the outer noise where they dance "freely," however, their so-called freedom only lasts for as long as the lights are on and for as long as the crowd gathers. When the lights are off, when the crowds go home, these people are left to their own silence and their silence is a place that they do not recognize, they do not know well, they do not belong to or inside of! There is no freedom. There is no freedom where man is not master of his own silence, where woman cannot be serene in her own awareness of her own self! When one is not master, is not mistress— one is slave. If you are not the master of your own inner silence then you are slave to the noise that you call your own.

Our children today are being called by name, into the noise, every day. Social media, pretentious friendships, false concepts and ideologies— all are lies that call our children by name. Our children login to Facebook and feel like they need to keep up with everybody else's "happiness", they login to Instagram and feel like they need to live a life for all to see, as if life is only worth living for the purpose of showing! Societal norms and ideologies, all the noise screaming in the computer screen and in the magazines and at school— all of this noise and more, they are the things that try to master our children, the things that would like to be master of our children (and of us).

The intimacy of existence is a very sacred thing. In this day and age, the sanctity of all things sacred is leveled out by the presentation of false pleasure coming from their exact opposites. To exist is a relationship, a reality; a relationship and a reality that is sacred, that is pure and that is holy. Our children are taught the whoredom of this most sacred thing. Our children are taught that to exist they must create something as an extension of themselves and present that thing to their friends, to the world! In this act alone, their existence begins to deteriorate. The sacred temple within themselves, where they truly exist, is being forgotten; *they* are forgetting their own true voice, their own true songs! Their songs are being blended into and overrun by all the noise! Their individual songs that they used to sing so confidently are becoming the song of their favourite celebrity, the song of their peers, the song of the popular kid on Facebook, the hymn of the most popular Instagram account! Where has the song of your daughter gone to? Why can you no longer remember the lyrics to your son's hymn?

I tell myself all the time, that to simply be on
Facebook, I need to have a very strong core, I need to
know that my core is a firm foundation, I need to
memorize the lyrics to my inner hymn, every day, so
that when I go onto Facebook and see everything in my
timeline from friends and from family, from strangers
and from companies, from groups and from
communities— I will not be quickly moved by the
sentiments that they want me to feel; but I will remain
within my own sphere of thought and feeling,
immoveable and unfazed! Indifferent and impenetrable.
Because much of what we face, every day, is a barrage of
attempts to influence us. It seems like everything wants
to influence us into feeling this way or that, into
thinking this way or that, into believing this way or the
other way! We have to be indifferent, we have to be
immoveable. We have to move our own souls, stir our
own souls at our own will, be masters and mistresses of
our own minds, bodies and spirits! This is a daily battle,
which I face and I am determined to be victorious at,
every day! But what if I didn't know that this battle is
raging? What if I *wasn't* determined? What if I didn't
know what and how to explain this to my own child, to
my own son? What would happen? I would lose my
song, that's what would happen. And my son would
most probably lose his own song, too! We would forget
the lyrics to our inner hymns, we would dance in the
light and in the outer music that is being played by a
jukebox over which we have no control! It's someone
else's jukebox! It's someone else's music, someone else's

rhythm, lyrics, music and style! It wouldn't be our own.
We would dance while the music plays and while the
people are around but then when the sun sets, we would
cower in our own darkness, not knowing our own
hallways, our own doors, our own rooms and windows
and walls! We wouldn't recognize our own ballroom.
We wouldn't know where we keep the candles and the
matches (or where the light switches are!)

I want to raise a son who knows how to hear the
lyrics to his own hymn even when the outside music is
playing! I want to raise a son who can hum and sing his
own song and dance to his own tune even while the
music from outside is playing! I want to give the gift of
impenetrability to my son and to myself, so mote it be.
And I want him to know the layout of his own ballrooms
so when the sun sets and the people go home, he will
know how to turn the chandeliers on! He will know how
to dance in the ballroom of his own mind, his own soul;
dance to the music of his own spirit, his own heart! I
want him to know how to turn on all of his chandeliers
and I want him to know where he's kept the candles and
the matches just in case! And I want the same for myself.
I want the same for you too, for you and your children.
So may God help us all.

Let us show our children not the need to be "nice"
and to be "likeable" but let us show our children the need
to be indifferent to what is not worthy of their inner
songs. Let us exemplify the need to be strong, the need
to be noble, the need to be master and mistress of our
own beings, our own minds, our own souls. Teach your

children how to build castles within them, how to open the windows inside of them, how to dine on banquets that take place within.

They Search For Fame

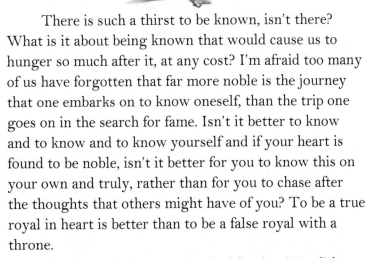

There is such a thirst to be known, isn't there? What is it about being known that would cause us to hunger so much after it, at any cost? I'm afraid too many of us have forgotten that far more noble is the journey that one embarks on to know oneself, than the trip one goes on in the search for fame. Isn't it better to know and to know and to know yourself and if your heart is found to be noble, isn't it better for you to know this on your own and truly, rather than for you to chase after the thoughts that others might have of you? To be a true royal in heart is better than to be a false royal with a throne.

The thirst for honey mixed with wine (Mead) has been forgotten in favour of the thrill of chasing after dirty water. Mead only comes from the places of highest magic; while dirty water is everywhere! Why are the children incapable of seeing what is better? Why do they chase after things of no worth? To have fame is not a sin and is not a folly; but it is of no worth if it is false. What is fame if it is fame in itself? Fame for what? Fame for simply being known? What are you known for and how did you become it? And if you were granted a good name and a good heart at birth then thank the gods for that; but if not, then do you suppose that taking up a false seat is better? And why would you covet what belongs to another? All that belongs to another belongs to him for a reason you do not know, and your business is to look upon yourself and be happy for others, for what they have and seek to know yourself and what your gifts are!

We forget that there are legions of witnesses. We never go unwatched. We forget that man is the least of these witnesses; that we are seen by the stars and the Moon and the Sun! We are seen by all that breathes that is beyond our eyes and just beyond our sense of touch! We seek too much to be witnessed by the eyes of mankind; forgetting that each step we take leaves a footprint for all the gods and angels to see! And happenchance we might leave our footprints embedded upon the skin of God, Himself. And yet too often, all that they care about is their neighbor, the person across the street, the people in school, the people at work, the people on their Facebook friends' list! Brother and sister! You are not forgotten! You are not small! And yet you seek a small audience, an audience that will soon fade away! For whom do you live your lives? For the mortals? For the memories of others instead of the memories that you will carry with you in your own minds and hearts? Do you want to be remembered by gods and angels? Or by man and woman? But who the gods remember— all will remember! To be remembered by the Heavens is to forget to care so much about what other people might think about you. Your Earthly legacy is in the hands of Divine Providence and while you keep your gaze upwards, there will your direction be also.

The constellations and the planets look upon the one who has mastered and known himself, the one who drinks Mead that is born of his own soul! Our children must see this life as a beautiful gift, as a place they have been given the chance to enjoy and to know themselves in! There should be no place, no space for debauchery, for the seeking of anything that is less!

Mead is the drink of the gods from the Yggdrasill (Tree of Life) in the spiritual belief system called *Ásatrú*, which hails from Norse legend and lore.

A Smile From Your Soul

Someone once said, "A woman should have two things: A smile and a guy who inspires it." But I think a woman should have a smile and a soul inside herself that inspires it.

As I write this, I find myself remembering what my mother used to say to me, "Everything you do to beautify yourself— your choice of clothing, makeup, what you do with your hair and how you walk and smile— don't do that for men or for a man. Do that because it makes you happy and make sure you're doing it because it makes you happy." She really only needed to tell me once, because I'm the kind of person who's just like that naturally, anyway. I grew up as a young girl doing things for my beauty that made *me* happy. My choice of clothing, the colours I wore, the things I did with my hair, the pair of jeans I picked out and the lip gloss that I wore— I had *myself* in mind. These things made *me* happy. Because what was important to me was that when I got home at the end of the day, I was happy with my day, happy with myself, it was important to me that the material things that I added to my life were being added to my life because they added to my happiness; not because I needed those material things in order to recruit other people into liking me and thus recruit happiness into my life as if joy is found riding on the backs of other people.

I believe that young girls and women everywhere should know that their beauty isn't a gift to the world; but that their beauty is a gift to themselves. Yes, the world may come to admire that beauty and there would be nothing wrong with that; but no matter what— she must first know that her beauty and that everything she does for it, is a gift for herself, a gift for her own soul.

Many people have an estranged relationship with material things. They designate people who glean happiness from material things as "materialistic" and then they draw this very thick line between people who are beautiful "on the outside" and people who they deem are most beautiful "on the inside." But the fact is that we are also corporeal beings and we live in a corporeal world and the key is actually to realize, know and be aware of the fact that what is material should serve our souls well; instead of taking over our mind, our spirit. The material things that you add to your life should serve the purpose of enlivening your soul. If it enlivens your life because it makes you happy, because it shows you more of yourself and your own beauty and purpose— that is a beneficial material thing. From this you can see how I chose to add material things to my life— they were added into my life to enliven my soul's experience here on Earth. After all, our lives in this corporeal world are gifts unto us! I believe we should choose to vivify our soul's experience, with things both corporeal and incorporeal, with the corporeal always serving its purpose to exhilarate the soul. I am very thankful to God for every material thing that I have and I see these all as gifts from Above!

The smiles on our faces must not depend on the people we are able to rake into our lives or even to keep in our lives; but our smiles must depend on the condition of our own souls and everything we do for ourselves must truly be for ourselves, not to please others or to make others like us. After all, the most important person you need to impress is yourself! The most important temple that you will ever build is not a temple that all the world may come to seek refuge in; but the most important temple that you will ever build is the temple that is you, one that you can seek refuge in, one that you have fortified and adorned.

Odinn's Son

The Ásatrú Edda: Sacred Lore of the North, by *The Norroena Society,* is the sacred text of *Ásatrú,* a Norse spirituality/belief system pre-dating Christianity. There is a particular verse taken from a personal conversation that the God Óðinn (Odinn) was having with his son, Höðr (Hoder), in which Odinn says, "Be not a shoemaker, nor a shaftmaker, unless it is for yourself, for a shoe if ill-made or a shaft if crooked will call evil down on you." There is another version of this online, which words that verse like this, "Be not a shoemaker nor yet a shaft maker save for thyself alone: lest the shoe be misshapen, or crooked the shaft, and a curse on thy head will be called."

It is often said that the problems we have in life arise from having too many vices; however, in my life, I have come to learn that the problems that I have had, have always, all the time, arisen from my vast stock of too many virtues. Born into a Christian (very Christian) family and named after two "most virtuous" virtues found in the Bible, I was raised (strictly raised) to see myself as a vessel unto honour, and by "vessel unto honour" what they meant was, a vessel of selfless service unto others, putting myself second to everyone else around me, seeing myself as less worthy than others around me, always looking inside myself to find what I could bring out of me to give to other people! I was definitely taught to see myself as both a shoemaker and a shaftmaker, to see myself as the server, as "the least of men." This was, according to "them", the most virtuous way to live one's life in honour of God. As a result, well, I am sure that anyone can easily imagine what kind of troubles I faced due to this mindset I carried around inside of my head! For one, I was an easy target at school since I was considered by many to be "the prettiest girl at school" and it was just their lucky day, every day, that "they" could actually mistreat and hurt that girl whenever they wanted to. It must feel so wonderful to be able to easily hurt the person that you envy the most! And what that overflow of virtue did for me, at the end of the day, was put me in a susceptible position open to feelings of resentment, revenge and inadequacy. I, however, do not blame the Christian beliefs for that outcome; but I acknowledge the possible unfortunate outcomes of choosing to bind the heart to all of its laws. After all, the greatest law above all other laws, is Freedom!

In *Divergent*, a recent novel by the American author Veronica Roth, society is divided into distinct factions by which people are placed according to their individual aptitudes, values, traits. Those factions are: Candor (the honest), Erudite (the intelligent), Amity (the peaceful), Abnegation (the selfless), and Dauntless (the brave). When the young ones reached a certain age to mark their maturity, they would be given the freedom to choose a faction different from the one they were born into. If I were a character in this novel, or rather, if this novel were real and we were all characters in it, I most surely would have been born and raised in Abnegation! Then later I am sure I would choose Dauntless. But I'm certain that I would know my true nature to be Divergent. Divergent is an outlawed group of individuals who exhibit all traits or at least more than one trait designated to and exemplified by the factions. They are outlawed and hunted down to death because they are a threat to the power of the system and to the reigning class (there is, at any given time, a reigning faction handling the power over the whole system.) I am sure I would be Divergent; not because the story is all about Divergents and just like any other audience member I would like to consider myself as the hero; not because of that, rather, because I know for a fact that I do exhibit all of those disparate factions within me and it really does show. And that isn't something I am saying to impress anyone; rather, I am saying that it is actually very difficult to exhibit strong aptitudes and traits shoved into gear by any circumstance at hand in order to make the best possible outcome of each! It is very difficult because people will not be able to "place" you and you will find it most difficult to "place" yourself, too! Different situations in life, even menial and daily tasks in life, call for different aptitudes, values, reactions, traits and characteristics in order for you to make the best out of those situations. And sometimes your different traits can express themselves very strongly, starkly in contrast to a trait you needed to exhibit in another situation just earlier, so on and so forth. And so it is difficult to be rare, It is difficult to be Divergent. I once wrote something, quite a long time ago, which I believe accurately describes the sentiment I'm trying to get across to you: "Lots of people are born into lives that feel like a journey in the very middle of a big ship on familiar seas; they sit comfortably, crossing their legs, they know when the sun will rise and when the moon will wane, they have plans that they follow, they have a map! But then there are those of us, a few, who are born into lives that feel like standing at the very top of the ship's stern; we have to stand up, hold on tight for dear life, we never know when the waves will rock and we never know where the sun will set or when the moon will wane! Nothing follows the laws of common nature and we live in a wild, wild awakening and the only map we have is the map of the stars! We're called to see the lighting tear at the horizon, we're chosen to roar with the tempests, but we're also the first ones to see the suns rise, the first ones to watch the moons form anew! There is nothing ordinary, nothing at all. But neither are we! And we wouldn't want it any other way!"

Many of us bring our children into the world and raise them in this society within the confines of our own factions that we were born into and belong to, ourselves. And that is okay, that is normal. But what if your child is Divergent? Are you going to cut him/her down? Turn off his/her spark? Are you going to teach your children that the other factions are lesser or are wrong?

In my case, I was not destined to be Abgnegation and not being allowed to be Divergent caused me a lot of pain early on in life, especially with the particular virtues of selflessness and service in question. You see, it is the nature of the ordinary human being to find fault in what he has been indulged into and familiarized with. I have my own examples of experiences to give but the one that can illustrate my point very simply and vividly, would be an experience I had with my classmate in high school. She used to hitch a ride in my car on her way home every day because otherwise, she would need to take public transportation. I happily let her ride with me every afternoon after school, dropping her off at her place each day. Until the time came when I couldn't let her ride with me just one afternoon and the very next morning, to my surprise, we weren't friends anymore! Not only would she not even talk to me anymore, but she actually went around spreading rumors about me! I have experienced numerous similar scenarios, all of which have given me a good look at this deeply seated bad character present in the human nature.

If you rip your skin off for your friend every day in order to clothe his flesh, bones and veins, you had better be ready for that same friend to curse you and say all manner of vile, evil things about you when the day comes that you will be needing your skin to clothe your own flesh, bones and veins! If you are going to give of yourself to other people, you had better be ready to be ridiculed and forgotten on the day that you need to keep yourself, for yourself! If you are going to be your best for another, you had better be ready to be cursed down to hell on the day that you cannot be your very best for him/her! Because that's how ordinary people are, and sweetheart, /I'd say 99% of people on this planet are ordinary. If you belong to the remaining percentage, you'd better not be a shoemaker or a shaftmaker. It's another story if the 99% were to become shoemakers and shaftmakers (would serve one another selflessly) because then that would change the nature of humankind. But that's not going to happen, at least not in this world! After all, this piece of advice from *The Ásatrú Edda* was given by a God, to a God!

Serve yourself and readily forgive yourself when your service to your own life experiences a flaw, an imperfection. Don't curse yourself to hell when you find a mistake in your own work, in your own creations in life. Practice your crafts in life with much care, seriousness and pleasure, whilst being quick to forgive yourself, quick to appreciate yourself and quick to see things that are wrong, for the purpose of fixing. Rejoice in any of your faults, for they only mean you are becoming better! Do not deny yourself the joy of finding the things that are wrong with you; but readily see those things and allow them to fade into nothingness. In that same light, do not deny yourself the knowledge of your beautiful truths, your beautiful forms, the beautiful shapes of your existence!

If only *Divergent* were a real story and we were all able to identify each other according to our factions, that would make our lives a whole lot easier, in a sense. We would be able to understand one another immediately due to our expectations being right on track from the very beginning. We would only judge others based upon their factions and not based upon our criticisms of each of their personalities. And in the midst of this, we would come to see that the one virtue really worth living by, is the acceptance of others. Because truly, all we really need to live by is the principle of not looking to find fault in others, not looking to weigh or measure ourselves up against the other, not comparing our progress or our worth to another's. All else are shoes and shafts.

A Secret Way

To forget a good deed done for you is the most shameful of acts you could do. I want to be remembered as someone who repays good with good, not as someone who forgets the kindness shown to her. And yet, here I am surrounded by a race of people that can easily repay good with evil and, that many times, will even see goodness as an easy way to get away with an evil! I was born into a world wherein every person and every object has the potential of hurting me, and worse, has the potential of distorting my view of myself. Because true demise comes about in one's life when his/her vision of his/her self becomes twisted, becomes distorted.

There is a rule which I teach my son to live by, and that is to never forget an act of kindness done towards him, to repay that act of kindness as much as he can. But because we live in a world where trust is a very scarce commodity, I also teach him to not attach feelings and emotions to this creed; but to simply live by this creed because it is an honourable way of being. Too much of the time, a person can be so eager to attach beautiful feelings to other people's actions and to his/her own reactions. And sometimes, that is only because a person is born with much beauty is his/her heart, thus beauty is laced by this individual around most of what happens to him or to her and also around most of what he or she does in return. But this beautiful, high-vibrational way

107

of being is attacked by the low-vibrational frequencies emitted by many people of the world and unfortunately it acts like rust upon a beautiful metal! Too many people of beautiful character slowly languish in a world filled with spiritual carcinogenic. The solution? There is no need to distribute oneself and one's way of being upon all other creatures and all other things! It is in fact more beneficial to act out of honour instead of from a well of deeply rooted emotional fingerprint. When you take from your heart to respond to everything and to everyone, you are lacing your heart around everything and everyone and this is of course a very sweet way of being; however, it is also a way of being that will prove non-beneficial for yourself in the end. And so I teach myself and my son to perform actions from honour instead of from the heart. The heart must be saved for only a few, including oneself.

My son is often trusted by school authorities to make reports on incidents coming from the least judgmental, least emotional perspective around. When people get into fights, so on and so forth, the school guidance counselor trusts the word of my son to report what really happened without any personal bias, without any personal judgment on either party and without a highly emotionally-charged state of being. This character of my son is something that developed without my particular incentive or awareness, I suppose it is his own character, all his own. I am inspired by this and I can see the benefit that stems from his way of being. He is able to somehow remove himself from the surface of things, remain in a state of indifference and see things simply for what they are whilst being able to give accurate narratives about what happens.

I believe that there are some children born into the world who have come here to love and to give, only to have their hearts torn apart again and again. Their good is responded with harm and their gentleness with suffering. This is wrong. And I know that some doctrines and some people may teach that this is an ideal and a holy way of being; but I disagree with that notion. To languish under heartache, no matter how wonderful a "sacrifice" it is for the rest of the world, is not in the interest of your own destiny, is not in the interest of your own dreams and your own life! For how does it profit a man if he gains the whole world but does not gain joy in his own soul? Let us not allow our children to languish under the performance of sacrifice; but sacrifice should be made through conscious efforts, for the edification of one's character. Sacrifice should not be something that is unfortunately wrought upon a person's soul due to the beautiful nature of that person's being!

A good deed done for you, no matter how small, should never be overlooked and never be forgotten. The good deeds of friends should be repaid with equal (or more) good, so long as one is physically and mentally capable of doing so. If one is not capable mentally and physically, such a person should not be ashamed of accepting good deeds done for him/her, even if he/she is not capable of repaying— for this is where grace comes into the picture. It is graceful to be able to receive and be thankful, even when one is not capable of giving the same to the other. But where one is capable, one must always repay an act of goodness with an equal or greater goodness, not because of emotional reasons but only because this is the only honourable thing to do with a goodness done unto you. Goodness forgotten and knowingly not repaid will turn into molds and mildew that gnaw at the finery of your existence and you never want that to happen to you.

They Say All is Fair in the Game of Love and War

I always tell my son that the one thing people do that can guarantee them retribution from higher powers— is deliberately taking another person's affections lightly. I have seen this time and time again. When it comes to romantic affections between two people, it seems like God takes a step back and hands you over to life itself and in the event you do not show respect and care for the other person's affections towards you— you have set in motion a special kind of "retribution" on behalf of the other person, against yourself! It always comes back to you and you always find yourself sitting in the corner, saying, "What I'm going through right now is definitely because of how I treated that person."

I don't know what it is about romantic feelings between two people that causes God to take a step back and let you do things on your own, but it seems to be just like that. When it comes to the hearts of other people and their romantic desires and passions for you, life demands that you show respect for that person's feelings. If not, well, life has a way of listing down such instances and coming back to hit you in the face with that list, in the future. And that is precisely why I often remind my son to always show respect towards any girl who likes him and that doesn't mean he has to like her back but that just means he has to honour her feelings

by not taking advantage of those feelings and by not
mocking those feelings or making her look desperate or
pitiful for having them.

The reason why we all tend to disrespect people
who like us, is unbeknownst to me. But it seems like we
are conditioned to play a game and the one who feels the
less is the one who is winning. Or the one who gets the
"last laugh" is the one who's won the game. What have
the people of the world done to human affections that it
has been painted in such a shade of ridicule and trickery?
We are not placed into life in order to play a game of
capturing people's affections and then throwing them
into some kind of a net along with fish and other things!
We are not placed into life in order to play a game of
love and war. There is something very volatile about the
affections of people and that volatility can very easily
turn against you for the worst, depending on how you
react to such feelings given to you by other individuals.
One must never lead another into hoping for something
that will never be; but on the other hand, one must also
never damn a person's feelings just because they are not
reciprocated. Furthermore, a person needs to handle
those feelings with care, dealing with them in the most
respectful of ways. Why? Because if not, life will really
get you for it. Given that it's a God-free zone, in a way,
and that you are on your own in this one, you've got to
take it upon yourself to really handle these matters with
utmost consideration and care. At the end of the day,
you are looking out for your own heart in the process.

Dear Darling,

"Don't let anyone make you become like them."
That is what I would say to my much younger self. If
there is any piece of advice I would like to give to her
(my much younger self) that would be it.

I wasted so much time and so many tears on people
who were able to pull me out of my own persona,
making me become like them. We take on the spots of
those whom we need to fight; leaving us more like them,
empty of the person that we really are!

I have always been predisposed to spontaneous
laughter, much like a little child is. This has been one of
my most enviable treasures throughout my life. In the
blink of an eye, there is a burst of unplanned innocence
and simple delight that just explodes into the air and I
see the changes that happen on the faces of certain folks
around me with less-than-noble intent! People are given
a sudden glimpse into what they really want— the
untainted joy of youth! But I was raised to be self-
degrading (something they called "humility") and I
never was really able to appreciate about myself, the
many things within me that people envied. I was always
focused on *giving myself* to people, without being armed
with the knowledge that more often than not (at least in
my life), people only want to take, take, take and that
means that you are not supposed to be focused on giving

yourself to the rest of the world; but you are supposed to be focused on seeing yourself and growing in the love that your life will allow you to know!

There was this one serious, difficult, unfortunate event in my life that finally woke me up to this. It was a painful experience that would not leave me affording to put aside my own happiness, to not appreciate my own nature and my own possessions. I'm going to avoid dropping names here, but I once met a prominent, famous woman. A socialite. She was around my age, very wealthy, cared for, pampered and all that. So I was having a conversation with her over some food and she said something which humoured me, thus throwing me into my childish bouts of laughter, and I saw her face, I saw her reaction! I understood that look on her face; I recognized it and I knew what it was. It was as if she had shriveled up in the matter of a second! Like if she were a grape, she had become a raisin in the snap of a finger! My delight and joy was like an airborne poison to her and I could just feel her envy seeping through the ground on which she stood! I could feel her thinking about all that she *didn't* have, when she saw my own nature, *just because she saw my own nature.*

What followed was something that I wish I could delete from my life, but on the other hand, I am thankful for the result of it, being that I was able to finally throw my lack of self-value out of the door. Without going into much detail of how or why this all unfolded, I will just say that she began to provoke me in a series of ways that I tried to ignore, but couldn't. And instead of clinging to my own nature, onto my own joy, I went out of my inner garden, into her valleys, where I was thoroughly stripped of my happiness for a much longer time than I deserved. Now, had I been able to keep my vision steady upon myself, upon my own visions, nature, dreams, upon nurturing the garden within me— I would have had the mind to simply turn my back on her, in favour of myself and my own well-being, hence avoiding the pitfalls that followed. That woman later exercised all of her prosperity and influence to oppress my family and me, because I had been provoked to a point where I fought back and said hurtful things to her. Of course, she took the opportunity to make my family and I suffer as a result of her feeling hurt. But at the root of all that suffering I experienced, was a person (me) who didn't know how to value the good things about her enough to know that she should *never* let *anyone* pull her into their valleys and make her like them! You see, when people envy you, they seek a perverse kind of "justice" against you, which is actually not "justice," at all! All they see are the things about you that they wish they had or that they wish they could be like and from then on they plot how to make things "even." They do a certain form of dark sorcery with fate and they attempt to twist or to remove these things about you that they envy. Some will simply backbite you in an attempt to remove what they envy in you from the view of others around, while others (who are more powerful or influential than the average person) will actually go to the extent of hurting not only you but the people that you love, too. Anything to rid themselves of the "unfairness" that they feel pervades their existence, because of your existence!

The best thing to do is to avoid and to walk away. The best way to avoid and the best way to walk away, is by entering into your very own inner garden. Marcus Aurelius, the Roman, Stoic Philosopher, Father, Warrior and Lover, was fond of reminding himself and his followers that the best true and lasting "getaway" for anyone, is not somewhere far away that one needs to arrive at by traveling; but that the true and lasting, always- present getaway is within one's own soul. According to him, if you are capable of entering therein at any needed time, you have truly attained mastery over your own soul. Emperor Marcus Aurelius once said, "Men seek retreats for themselves, houses in the country, sea-shores, and mountains; and thou too art wont to desire such things very much. But this is altogether a mark of the most common sort of men, for it is in thy power whenever thou shalt choose to retire into thyself. For nowhere either with more quiet or more freedom from trouble does a man retire than into his own soul."

Why do people run away from situations, only to find themselves running into the same dead ends along the new paths that they turn to? Well, that is because all conflict is really carried around on the inside and not really on the outside. The conflicts that we have in life that we can touch and see are mere results of conflicts within. And that is why we must learn to *"run away within."* We must learn to be far, far away from our enemies, even when we don't have the choice or the power to run away from them physically. Just think, if I had retreated to where I would be truly safe inside my inner garden that is crawling with climbing roses and their sweet scents— then I would have been able to avoid the greater sorrow that I didn't foresee! The greater sorrow caused by someone who was cunning, manipulative and envious.

Too often in my life, my goal has been to be sincere and I have been just that— to a fault! To a fault that I wish I never had to experience. In fact, this is one of the most difficult and greatest of lessons that I have learned in my life, taking me numerous experiences of similar nature before I was finally capable of ridding myself of it. We think too often that we need to show our utmost sincerity to the world so that we can save them, so that we can be good or better people, so that we can be virtuous! But I have learned from the teachings of no less than the Norse God, Heimdallr, "The immortal among mortals, the guest among men, the companion of humans" who once said, "Without freedom, all other virtues are good only to make you into slaves, your heritage to everlasting shame." Without the freedom to be happy, to run from those who wish us harm, to turn our backs against those with less than worthy intentions towards us— it really doesn't matter if our own intentions are that of utmost sincerity and virtue and honesty and bravery— because we are in the end left in the dust as slaves! Especially if those who provoke us have power over us because of their wealth and status in society!

There is an all-encompassing beauty in the innocence of lacking the need to express our virtues! When we realize that our virtues can be nurtured just for our own happiness and for the happiness of our loved ones, that truly sets us free! And so it is actually the state of being bound by our virtues that many times causes us to fall victim to others who would entrap us in order to try and make us like them, in order to try and level their playing field! If I had not been so sincere, seeing myself as needing to be brave and needing to correct other people's wrongdoings, then I would not have even bothered to set that particular person straight, I would not have been sincere with my intentions and emotions towards her from the very beginning and I would not have seen it needful to take on her provocations and then later to fight her.

Because of a simple joyous laughter striking envy in the heart of one who had the means to oppress other people, I experienced the fear for my life and the life of my family members. This is a somber thought, it really is. Had I been aware of the worth of my nature, had I been free from the need to be virtuous and stand my ground to fight, had I been more interested in my own happiness rather than in going out into inner valleys of someone else, only to be mobbed by them, had I known all of this back then; I would have been able to avoid a very, very difficult time in my life! So this is a very valuable lesson that I pass on to my son and to you who are reading this.

Always remember that you never need to save anyone with your virtues, you never need to give of yourself to the world, you never need to see less of the worth of your beautiful qualities just to "be humble." You never need to lose your happiness and become like somebody else. You never need to allow anybody to ever do that to you, to ever pull you out of yourself and make you into something that resembles them. Retreat into the garden that is within and there be innocent, there be void of charity, of selflessness, of virtue! There be enswathed in the dewdrops of the beautiful natures of your own spirit. Please be well, darling. Please be happy and laugh and never let *anyone* take that away from you!

"Honor that which is the best in yourself."
(Emperor Marcus Aurelius, *Meditations*)

"Above all things reverence thyself.
Above all things, respect thyself.
Above the cloud with its shadow is the star with its light.
Above all things reverence thyself."
— Pythagoras of Samos

The Unpolished Stone of Immense Worth

I was raised in a very religious home where happiness was considered to be a "lesser" state of being. In fact, my dad wouldn't even allow me to use the word "happy" and I was only allowed to use the word "joy" to describe my mirth or delight! As a result, I grew up not being allowed to search for happiness, I was told that "life is pain" and when it came to love, relationships, how I spent my time, so on and so forth, I wasn't allowed to do any of those things for the goal of being happy. I was taught to always ask, "Why am I doing this? Is it the right thing to do? Will it honour God? Will it make *God* happy?" You see, when it came to God's happiness, it was okay; but when it came to *my* happiness, that was just unholy and out of the question! And I believe that it is because of this upbringing that life has put me through serious events that have forced me to grasp for happiness. Through my past misfortunes, I have come to shun the toil for too much virtue, I have come to know that happiness is indeed a simple thing; but that being simple doesn't exactly mean being "less" or being "not good enough." I have in fact come to love what is simple, like happiness, and I have been taught by life to look for it in all things!

Now I believe that happiness is the holy grail of life. Why should you do something? You should do something when it is beneficial to you and if it will make you happy. People of many virtues perhaps do not understand this mindset; but I, coming from a place of incredibly and overly lofty virtues, can say that those who do destructive things do not do them because those things make them "happy." As a matter of fact, destruction is performed in the wake of the flight of happiness and by "flight" I mean "departure." People are not going to hurt people and destroy things or themselves because it makes them happy! No, people do those things when they are the furthest from happiness! No, your kids are not going to do drugs because it makes them happy; they will most likely do drugs if they have no inner strength and sense of self-worth enough to know that they should not feel any pressure whatsoever to do whatever it is that their friends or peers are doing just because they want to feel like they "belong." Your kids are not going to become promiscuous because it makes them happy; they are going to become promiscuous if they lack the knowledge of the value of developing the threefold mastership within themselves, when they lack the awareness of what it means to possess the power of mind over the desires of flesh! Your kids are not going to steal other people's things because it makes them happy; no, but they might steal other people's things if they don't understand the value of people's possessions and material things and why those objects should not be taken away from others!

Happiness is the simple state of being that is often shunned by those on a presumably "higher" path or calling. In other words, the self-righteous. Self-righteousness, after all, is the enemy and the deadly poison of the human body, mind and spirit. To be a fault-finder is to be a disease-ridden body, to be a judger of others' lives is to be a mind plagued by unseen darkness, to be a condemner is to be a soul that condemns its own self to grief!

I can see how I have failed numerous "tests" I was given in life, simply by failing to be happy! There is a variety of circumstances wherein I was blessed exceedingly and yet due to my overtly virtuous nature, I failed to simply see the blessings that I had, I failed to simply be happy! Time and time again, more and more was given to me and yet, I failed again and again! I failed because I could not reach down to the level of happiness, while I was too busy reaching up high for the levels of "what was right." But isn't it in the bending down to reach what is lower that we are expressing a true form of humility? Isn't it humility to be okay with reaching for what is deemed as lesser? And isn't it humility to be okay with belonging to what is seen to be of smaller virtue?

Much was taken away from my life, so that I might finally be happy, so that I might finally grasp for what I could find on the ground in the hole that I fell into! Can you guess what was there with me on the ground in that hole wherein I felt like God and all of His Angels had forsaken me completely? At the bottom of it all— I found happiness! Why? For no reasons at all! I found that I was able to be happy simply because happiness was with me down there on the ground, in the dirt, when all else that I once knew had abandoned me! Happiness was the naked dirt that I sat on! And I learned that in the absence of all the things that should have made me happy before— happiness was actually the one thing that I could hold onto! Being happy for no reason at all, just because I made the choice to be! I realized that I can be happy because of the wind, or because I am me!

The lessons that life gave me, in order to teach me the value of the simpler, non-profound asset called happiness, were very painful lessons that I would rather not have needed to experience. I know that if I had been allowed to pursue the rawest form of innocence— the experience of happiness— I wouldn't have ever needed to go through the crucibles that I endured. But then I am thankful because I realize that to Someone/ Some Beings out there, I am important enough to have been taught such lessons. I can now only be grateful and only remember the things that I have learned. I hope that you will, too.

Until next time!

Special Mentions

A big hug of gratitude for my copyeditor from Greece, Toula Fanariotou, who is also my good friend. I find it very amusing how my copyeditor is a non-native English speaker! Thank you for squashing the bugs in my manuscript, Toula mou! By the powers invested in you by Athena! S'agapou!

A special mention goes to *Oh So Nifty Vintage Graphics* for all the royalty-free, commercial use, public domain vintage book art, taken from very old manuscripts and made available for modern-day use, thanks to the generosity of the person running this particular project. http://vintagegraphics.ohsonifty.com/

Last but certainly not the least, I want to thank Corinne Knapp Rogers of *Hampton Photography NY*, for the two photos that grace the cover of this book and also for the titling design. I have been working with Corinne for a while now and together we have produced a variety of book covers for my own books. This one is extra special though, as it features Corinne's very own fiancé, Ronnie Russo, on the front cover, along with their son, Ronnie Jr. I'm sure you would agree that this book's cover is both stunning and memorable, which is testament to the talent of this superwoman! The back cover is graced by the magical Makenna Saige Monahan and the wonderful William Gavinovich.
www.hamptonphotographyny.com

Notes...

Notes...

The main typeface in this book is set in 12 pt. *Bell*, created by Richard Austin, for John Bell (owner of a British Letter Foundry), in 1788. *Bell* was considered to be the first real English Modern Face by one of the most influential type-designers of the 20'th century, Stanley Morison. It is also considered to be the earliest example of Scotch Roman Face.

I was previously unaware of the existence of this font and I discovered it simply by surprise! I thought, *what a perfect font for me to work with, it is my namesake!* So I tested it in this manuscript and found that the feeling of reading it was happy, open and joyous! I fell in love with this font for the feelings it gave me! It was able to make me feel *like me!* It made me feel like I was smiling and laughing! Now that's more than I can say about any other font I have worked with.